Michael Volland has been Direc Durham, since 2009. Since 2014, he has combined this role with serving as Missioner to nine parishes in the East Durham Mission Project. Michael holds a commission in the Royal Army Chaplain's Department and serves as chaplain to the Durham Army Cadet Force. He trained for ordained ministry at Ridley Hall, Cambridge and undertook his doctoral studies at Durham University. Michael has published a number of books, chapters and articles, including *Fresh! An Introduction to Fresh Expressions and Pioneer Ministry* (SCM Press, 2012); *Through the Pilgrim Door* (Survivor, 2009) and *God on the Beach* (Survivor, 2005). Michael is married and he and his wife have three children.

THE MINISTER AS ENTREPRENEUR

Leading and growing the Church in an age of rapid change

Michael Volland

First published in Great Britain in 2015

Society for Promoting Christian Knowledge
36 Causton Street
London SW1P 4ST
www.spckpublishing.co.uk

British Library Cataloguing-in-Publication Data
A catalogue record for this book is available from the British Library

ISBN 978–0–281–07182–1
eBook ISBN 978–0–281–07183–8

Typeset by Lapiz Digital Services
First printed in Great Britain by Ashford Colour Press
Subsequently digitally printed in Great Britain

eBook by Lapiz Digital Services

Produced on paper from sustainable forests

Contents

Contents

Introduction: Why 'entrepreneur'?

I am a Christian minister. I am also an entrepreneur. Being an entrepreneur has rarely made me any money and in the context of this book, that is precisely the point. Here I shall instead be using the term 'entrepreneur' to refer to a way of being in the world that is characterized by a relentless and energetic pursuit of opportunities to do things in new ways in order to bring about improvements for everyone involved.

Of course, some entrepreneurs act in this way in order to generate financial capital, but the work of the entrepreneur is not limited to the world of commerce. Entrepreneurs use their gifts in diverse environments including schools, hospitals and churches, and their efforts generate social, artistic and spiritual capital. My own entrepreneurial nature has found various expressions as an undergraduate art student, parish youth worker, budding author, mission-team member, ordained Anglican priest, lecturer in a theological college and missioner to a group of former mining villages in County Durham.

Being an entrepreneur is a fundamental aspect of my personality. I was never taught to be an entrepreneur but through establishing and running secret clubs and playground swap-shops at primary school, persuading a leading computer manufacturer to deliver a lorry-load of free equipment to my secondary school and establishing and running a successful club night as a young adult, I recognized my entrepreneurial flair, experimented with it, learnt from my mistakes and grew in entrepreneurial confidence. And once I was ordained in the Church of England it was natural to apply this 'way of being' to my approach to public ministry.

I did not mention entrepreneurship overtly during my selection process for ordained ministry, college training or deployment. However, my way of approaching the Christian life has always been innately entrepreneurial and I have tried to find creative and innovative ways to engage in loving service as a minister of the gospel in the communities in which I have served. My experience of being

1

an entrepreneurial minister (both lay and ordained) has been one of the key drivers for this book.

A second, intimately related driver has been my understanding of the nature of the mission context in which Christians are currently seeking to engage in faithful witness and loving service. Many years of involvement in, and reflection on, mission and ministry have led me to believe that today, the Church's faithful and effective response to Jesus' Great Commission requires the contribution of entrepreneurs.

How do you feel about entrepreneurs?

Consider the word 'entrepreneur', and note the sorts of images that come to mind. Is it a word you are comfortable with? Perhaps it is a word you instinctively recoil from. Maybe you are content for the word to be used in the world of commerce but the idea of its employment in relation to Christian ministry and mission raises all sorts of problems.

While the instinctive reaction of some Christians might be to steer clear of the word and its apparently worldly connotations, it is nevertheless true that we see many of the characteristics associated with entrepreneurship displayed in Christians who help to bring about imaginative change in communities and churches. I believe that entrepreneurship is a gift of God to his Church and that the Church and the communities it seeks to serve would gain a great deal if this gift were better understood and indeed encouraged. Not all Christians are natural entrepreneurs but many more than we imagine have the potential to be entrepreneurs, and when this potential is recognized, nurtured and given space to breathe, an innovative approach to mission and ministry is often the result.

A working definition of the entrepreneur

A few years ago I set about trying to find a definition of the entrepreneur that would provoke constructive discussion. It transpires that there is no widely accepted definition in the literature! What I noticed, however, as I read about entrepreneurs was the recurrence of words such as 'creative', 'innovative', 'energetic', 'focused', 'visionary', 'opportunity', 'partnership' and 'collaboration' – in short, all things that we might hope to see in those involved in Christian mission. With these concepts in mind, and drawing on the work of many others, I came up with the following definition of the entrepreneur:

> A visionary who, in partnership with God and others, challenges the status quo by energetically creating and innovating in order to shape something of kingdom value.

Visionaries are often able to see what *might* be, as well as what *is*. And, if they have wisdom and the ability to build trust and to communicate effectively, they may be able to share this vision with others and work in partnership to see it realized. Entrepreneurs' energy is often directed at moving beyond the status quo, or the apparent limits of the way things are. This can make them quite annoying to the rest of us! But for Christians, Jesus provides an example of someone who was prepared to disturb individuals and institutions where apathy and the love of comfort had crept in. Perhaps reflecting on Jesus' entrepreneurial approach to ministry may help us to recognize and celebrate the gift of entrepreneurship in our Christian communities. Considering entrepreneurship in the light of the definition set out above offers us a way of thinking about the task of mission to which God calls all of us and the kind of approach that some Christians might take towards it. I shall consider this definition in more depth in Chapter 2.

The aim of this book

This book aims to make a contribution to the emergence of a culture in which entrepreneurs and entrepreneurship are properly *understood* and *recognized* as gifts of God to his Church. As such a culture emerges, I hope Christians will feel more confident about acting out their God-given entrepreneurial potential and try out a whole range of experiments and innovations in local churches and communities.

Entrepreneurs have always been found among the people of God. Men and women with entrepreneurial gifts are present in the Bible and throughout church history. In predictable times, when the Church appears to be strong and affluent (never a great thing for the Church), the particular set of gifts possessed by the entrepreneurs in our midst are all too often ignored, discouraged or even repressed. During such times entrepreneurs appear to fade into the background. But in a challenging and unpredictable age like our own, it is important that the entrepreneurs among the people of God are given every encouragement to minister out of their God-given gifts. Part of the fruit of this will be that the rest of us are helped to step towards all that God intends and the unchanging message of the coming kingdom will be faithfully proclaimed in ways that allow it to be heard afresh in our generation.

This book is intended to be accessible to readers with a variety of needs and agendas, including lay and ordained ministers, church groups seeking resources to develop a more entrepreneurial approach to ministry, theological students studying entrepreneurial approaches to ministry and academics engaged in research.

Ministers and ministry

All Christians, by virtue of their baptism into the body of Christ, are called to be ministers of the gospel. Together, ours is a ministry of praise and worship, faithful witness, loving service, healing and reconciliation. Ministry involves working with one another to sustain and build up the body of Christ, while at the same time witnessing to the world in word and deed in order that others may have the opportunity to encounter the risen and ascended Jesus and be transformed by his love.

In the first instance, when I write about the 'minister', I am referring to *all* who have chosen to follow Jesus, and not only those who serve in leadership, teaching or sacramental roles. In using the word 'ministry', I am referring to a vast tapestry of activity that baptized Christians undertake in the name of Jesus and on behalf of his Church and not just to the narrower set of tasks undertaken by those in leadership roles. When I write about 'entrepreneurial ministers', then, I am first of all referring to Christians, whether in leadership roles or not, whose particular attributes we can recognize as being entrepreneurial and whose way of being in the world means that all manner of things happen that perhaps wouldn't have happened had God not placed them in our midst. Throughout the book I also make specific reference to 'lay' or 'ordained' entrepreneurial ministers. In Part 2 I focus specifically on ordained entrepreneurial ministers, as this has been the main focus of my own recent research.

4

Quality research requires a clear focus and this means imposing limitations on the scope of any particular project. As an Anglican involved in training men and women for ordained ministry, it made sense for me to focus in my research on *ordained Anglicans* exercising an entrepreneurial approach to ministry rather than those with leadership roles in other denominations. However, if the Church is to be blessed and encouraged by the ministries of *all* the entrepreneurs in our midst, of course we must identify, encourage and support entrepreneurial lay people. Among the myriad reasons for this is that those with entrepreneurial ability will often not be ordained clergy but lay ministers. Ordained ministers who understand the importance of creating an atmosphere in which entrepreneurial Christians can emerge and flourish will need to understand how to provide those Christians with appropriate support and guidance.

In his book, *Being Church, Doing Life*, Michael Moynagh highlights the important contribution that non-entrepreneurial pastors can make to facilitating the emergence of an entrepreneurial approach to ministry:

> You do not have to be an innovator yourself. You can be a pastor to those who are . . . You don't need to be a gifted change agent. Nor do you have to be gifted in up-front leadership to encourage these communities [and experiments].[1]

There is a great deal of work to be done on researching the contribution of lay entrepreneurs within the ministry of the Church and local communities and I hope that some readers will be able to engage in this much-needed task.

Why 'entrepreneur'?

I was talking about entrepreneurship at a conference and somebody asked me why I seemed to be hung up on using the word 'entrepreneur' rather than a term with less apparent baggage: something like 'innovator', 'creative person' or 'pioneer'. I explained that the word 'entrepreneur' catches up a whole range of qualities that no other word quite can.

---

[1] Michael Moynagh, *Being Church, Doing Life: Creating Gospel Communities Where Life Happens* (Oxford: Monarch Books, 2014), 240–1.

An effective entrepreneur may well be an innovator, but is *also* likely to be creative, energetic, a visionary, a collaborator and so on. 'Pioneer' doesn't quite capture the essence of the word 'entrepreneur' either. Although some pioneers have entrepreneurial qualities, not all pioneers are entrepreneurs. Some will blaze a trail once or even twice but may then stop pioneering and settle into other tasks. Entrepreneurs, on the other hand, do what they do again and again. Their approach to life and ministry is habitual and they can't help themselves. Doing new things in new ways is at the heart of their way of being in the world and they will go on seeing new or refreshed possibilities for people, places and things for the rest of their lives, and probably in the age to come! So the term 'entrepreneur' offers us a combination of qualities and gifts that no other word does.

'Entrepreneur' is also a word that appeared in direct relation to Christian ministry in a best-selling church report. In February 2004, the General Synod of the Church of England approved and commended the report, *Mission-Shaped Church* (*MSC*). The word 'entrepreneur' is used in the report's recommendations; specifically, Recommendation 11 states that 'those involved in selection need to be adequately equipped to identify and affirm pioneers and mission entrepreneurs'.[2] *MSC* assumes a link between 'mission entrepreneurs'[3] and the planting of fresh expressions of church, and specifies that the latter will be undertaken by the former.

Church planting is an important activity and *MSC* is right to highlight the need to identify individuals who have the gifts to undertake this task. However, the planting of contextual churches[4] by mission entrepreneurs is but one part of a much bigger picture. This book rests on the belief that entrepreneurs have a wider contribution to make to the task of mission and that it is important for the Church to

---

[2] Archbishop's Council, *Mission-Shaped Church: Church Planting and Fresh Expressions of Church in a Changing Context* (London: Church House Publishing, 2004), 147.

[3] *Mission-Shaped Church*, 147.

[4] Michael Moynagh uses the umbrella term 'new contextual church' 'to describe the birth and growth of Christian communities that serve people mainly outside the church, belong to their culture, make discipleship a priority and form a new church among the people they serve'. Moynagh identifies four overlapping responses to the new situation from which new contextual churches are emerging. These are: 'Church planting'; 'The emerging church conversation'; 'Fresh Expressions of church'; and 'Communities in mission'. Michael Moynagh, *Church for Every Context: An Introduction to Theology and Practice* (London: SCM Press, 2012), x–xiii.

recognize entrepreneurs who are engaged in ministry and mission and to encourage, support and learn from them. Understanding of the activities of the 'mission entrepreneur' should therefore be broader than the planting of new contextual churches and can in fact take in a whole range of activities undertaken by entrepreneurial Christians.

When I was first ordained I worked in Gloucester, where part of my role involved collaborating with ministers from a range of local churches. I quickly learnt to value the breadth of their activity and the potential for positive change that they could offer when adopting what might be described as an entrepreneurial approach to their ministries. This continued when I moved to Durham where, as a result of arranging student mission activity, I collaborated with ordained and lay ministers from various denominations. Here, once again, I was able to see the positive impact on local communities and congregations made by those who adopted an entrepreneurial approach to ministry and mission.

I am not suggesting that all Christian ministers or lay people are or should try to be entrepreneurs. Nor do I suggest that entrepreneurial ministers are the only solution to the numerical and financial decline some denominations face. I do suggest, however, that entrepreneurs can make a positive difference and are therefore a potential resource to our churches. According to the academics Bill Bolton and John Thompson, 'entrepreneurs create and build the future and they are to be found in every walk of life and in every group of people. Every community group, every public organization has within it an entrepreneurial potential.'[5]

Why now?

By the end of this book I hope to have convinced you that the answer to that question is that *entrepreneurs are a gift of God to the Church in a time of rapid and discontinuous cultural change.*[6]

---

[5] Bill Bolton and John Thompson, *Entrepreneurs: Talent, Temperament, Technique*, 2nd edn (Oxford: Elsevier, 2004), 1.

[6] In their book, *The Missional Leader: Equipping Your Church to Reach a Changing World* (San Francisco, CA: Jossey-Bass, 2006), Alan Roxburgh and Fred Romanuk point out that in contrast to 'continuous change', which develops out of what has gone before, 'discontinuous change' is disruptive and unanticipated, creating situations that challenge our assumptions and require different skills and ways of working (p. 7).

Building on the social, cultural, theological and ecclesiological case constructed by *MSC*, it is my contention that the language of entrepreneurship offers the Church a useful way of imagining the future shape of mission. I believe that lay and ordained ministers with active and innate entrepreneurial ability are present in all denominations of the Church and that they are a potential resource at a time when churches are seeking to address significant missional challenges.

How Christian ministry is exercised in every age depends in large part on how particular churches relate to Scripture, their own tradition and the wider culture within which they operate. The Church of England, for example, understands its relation to the wider culture primarily in the light of its dual calling: to worship God and to participate in and serve his mission in the world.[7] Within the wider culture the exercise of ministry will necessarily require certain gifts and competencies at particular times. Ministers who adopt an entrepreneurial approach to their ministries will be particularly useful in assisting the Church to be faithful to its missionary calling at the present time.

In seeking to understand the nature and scope of the task of mission, major denominations, including the member churches of the global Anglican Communion and the Methodist Church, draw on the Five Marks of Mission.[8] These are:

1 To proclaim the good news of the kingdom.
2 To teach, baptize and nurture new believers.
3 To respond to human need by loving service.
4 To seek to transform unjust structures of society.

---

[7] The report of the 1988 Lambeth Conference states that Anglican Christians 'follow Jesus who said, "As the Father has sent me, so I send you"' (John 20.21). We are called to serve God's mission by living and proclaiming the good news. 'It's not the Church of God that has a mission, but the God of mission who has a Church.' As we follow Jesus Christ, we believe that God's mission is revealed to us by the Holy Spirit in three ways: through the Bible, through the tradition and life of the Church, and through our own listening, praying, thinking and sharing as we respond to our own context.' Lambeth Conference 1998, Section II, 121. <www.cofe.anglican.org/faith/mission/missionevangelism.html> (24/01/13).

[8] The Anglican Consultative Council notes, 'The first mark of mission is really a summary of what *all* mission is about, because it is based on Jesus' own summary of his mission (Matthew 4:17, Mark 1:14–15, Luke 4:18, Luke 7:22; cf. John 3:14–17). Instead of being just one of five distinct activities, this should be the key statement about *everything* we do in mission.' <www.Churchofengland.org/our-faith/mission/missionevangelism.aspx> (24/01/13).

5 To strive to safeguard the integrity of creation and to sustain the life of the earth.

Undertaking the ministries outlined by the five marks assumes a people in movement and requires the courage to take risks, the ability to spot opportunities, the energy to be creative, the intelligence to innovate and the faith and vision to work for transformation in lives and communities. The entrepreneurial minister will, to varying degrees, possess some or all of these qualities, will set an example in putting them into practice and will encourage them within his or her congregation and community. The Anglican Declaration of Assent[9] is useful to us here. The Declaration is read out by the presiding bishop each time an ordained minister is licensed to a new parish. Of particular interest is the fact that it states plainly the need for the people of God to proclaim the Christian faith *afresh* in each generation. Newly licensed ministers are to commit themselves publicly to partnering with God and the people of God who are in their pastoral charge in the task of proclaiming the good news about Jesus Christ within the body and also, crucially, to those in 'each generation' – in other words, to those in surrounding communities.

In a post-Christian environment the task of proclaiming the gospel afresh is particularly challenging. Steven Croft, the Bishop of Sheffield, acknowledges this challenge and, because he implies change within the Church itself, his position highlights the importance of training, deploying and supporting lay and ordained ministers who are able to understand what is happening and respond appropriately:

> The forces of change that have been affecting our culture and society have to affect the whole way we are church; the way we engage as churches in the mission of God in our generation; and therefore the nature and task of those who are ordained ministers.[10]

To be faithful and effective in the present 'generation' every minister must understand the essence of the gospel; be actively committed to radical love and service; grasp the rich heritage of the Church;

---

[9] The Declaration of Assent includes the following statement: 'The Church of England professes the faith uniquely revealed in the Holy Scriptures and set forth in the catholic creeds, which faith the Church is called upon to proclaim afresh in each generation.' Canon C 15, <www.Churchofengland.org/media/35588/complete.pdf> (24/01/13).

[10] Steven Croft, *Ministry in Three Dimensions* (London: Darton, Longman and Todd, 2008), 5.

and be able to read the wider culture. The minister must also avoid simply acting as a translator standing in the gaps between these diverse elements, but should rather be a prayerful catalyst for bringing them together so that, under the guidance of the Holy Spirit, something new might be brought to birth. This 'new' thing will be consistent with what has gone before while being also appropriate for our time. This is where the entrepreneurial minister's God-given creativity will be seen to be at work in collaboration with the creative Spirit of God, who is always and everywhere doing a new thing.[11] The result of this creative collaboration will take many different shapes but will everywhere be characterized by positive transformation.[12]

Since entrepreneurs thrive in an environment characterized by change and fluidity, changing times in the Church and the wider culture represent opportunities for the entrepreneurial minister: opportunities to re-imagine[13] the shape and nature of the relationship between the people of God and the surrounding culture; opportunities to take risks re-imagining the nature of the Church; opportunities to re-imagine the way the good news about Jesus might be communicated and apprehended by local people and become a source of positive transformation for local communities in which people are struggling with the effects of social and economic deprivation.[14] Making a public commitment to work with the people of God in proclaiming afresh the Christian faith in our post-Christian, individualized, consumer-oriented, networked culture is a challenge that the entrepreneurial minister is well fitted to meet. Entrepreneurial ministers have a contribution to make to the whole Church as it attempts to discern the shape of its ministry and mission in the present and in the years to come.

---

[11] I note the words of Isaiah in relation to God's perpetual creative activity: 'See, I am doing a new thing! Now it springs up; do you not perceive it? I am making a way in the wilderness and streams in the wasteland' (Isaiah 43.19).

[12] 'For Anglican Christians God's mission is about transformation; transforming individual lives, transforming communities and transforming the world.' Lambeth Conference 1998, Section II p. 121, <www.Churchofengland.org/our-faith/mission/missionevangelism.aspx> (24/01/13).

[13] *MSC* argues that in a time of rapid cultural change, 'perhaps our greatest need is a baptism of imagination about the forms of the Church'. *MSC*, 90.

[14] In a chapter titled 'Imagination', Sam Wells argues that 'Imagination essentially means being able to conceive of a world different from this one. What was required was something to do (imagination) [and this] included education, entrepreneurship, confidence and resilience.' Sam Wells and Sarah Coakley (eds), *Praying for England: Priestly Presence in Contemporary Culture* (London: Continuum, 2008), 83.

An outline of this book

This book is divided into two parts. In Part 1 (Chapters 1, 2 and 3), I address the reservations some Christians have about the concept of entrepreneurship in relation to Christian ministry. I suggest that it is the association of entrepreneurs with the greed that largely defined the enterprise culture of the 1980s that Christians often struggle with, and that this association has given rise to a misconception of the entrepreneur as a 'lone wolf', making money at other people's expense. I consider an alternative understanding of the entrepreneur, showing that Christians who possess entrepreneurial character traits are a gift of God to the Church because they can imagine what might be, communicate this vision appropriately, and engage in genuine partnership with others in order to see new or improved outcomes, all for the sake of the coming kingdom of God. I propose that God demonstrates characteristics associated with entrepreneurship and that an entrepreneurial approach to ministry and mission is one that we are not only able to see in the Bible and Christian history but should expect to see in our own times too.

In Part 2, I briefly explain the approach I took to researching entrepreneurial ministers and then present six key findings that emerged from the research. Discussion of the findings is followed by some suggestions about what the Church can do to encourage a more entrepreneurial approach to ministry and mission.

At the end of the book there is an appendix offering chapter-by-chapter suggestions for group discussion. A second appendix provides suggested essay questions for students seeking to engage with the arguments in the general introduction and in the three chapters that form Part 1.

As I researched entrepreneurial ministers I built on the work of many others, and part of my intention in publishing my findings is that some readers will themselves be encouraged to contribute to the Church's understanding in this area by developing what is set out here and taking it in new directions. For such readers there is therefore a third appendix setting out suggestions for further research.

Part 1

ENTREPRENEURS: WHAT? WHO? WHY NOW . . .?

1

Dragons' Den? *Towards a positive understanding of the entrepreneur*

A contested term

The word, entrepreneur, draws a mixed response when it is used in conjunction with Christian ministry. Although some are happy with it, more often than not it prompts responses ranging from discomfort to fervent objection. No doubt this is due to the association of the word with a worldly approach to wealth creation for personal gain.[1]

I wrote these words in a chapter I contributed to a textbook on fresh expressions of church and pioneer ministry. The comment comes in the middle of a passage of reflection on the kind of approach to Christian ministry that might currently be necessary in the United Kingdom. I deliberately use the term 'entrepreneur' to prompt readers to consider the sorts of qualities that might be desirable in those engaging in this task. As part of my research for the chapter I invited 30 men and women who were each engaged in various forms of Christian ministry to complete a survey. They were asked to provide responses to a number of questions, among them the following: 'Comment on the use of the term "entrepreneur" in relation to Christian pioneering'.[2] The responses were interesting and varied, and I have reproduced nine of them below.[3]

---

[1] Michael Volland, 'God's Call to Pioneer', in David Goodhew, Andrew Roberts and Michael Volland, *Fresh: An Introduction to Fresh Expressions of Church and Pioneer Ministry* (London: SCM Press, 2012), 143.

[2] Volland, 'God's Call to Pioneer', 146.

[3] Volland, 'God's Call to Pioneer', 146–9.

John Went
Sometimes entrepreneurs have a tendency to be sole operators, not good at listening to others, so I would wish to qualify entrepreneur with the ability to listen and to collaboratively involve others in the mission task.

Chris Howson
I loathe the use of the term 'entrepreneur'. We do not need to borrow more terms from the market – our faith has been privatized enough as it is! The word entrepreneur has too many connotations with taking risks for personal gain. The risks that a Christian takes are at personal cost, not gain. If one looks at contemporary understanding of the entrepreneur it is associated with programmes such as *The Apprentice* and *Dragons' Den*. These programmes reflect the ruthlessness of modern capitalist society, and are inherently confrontational and combative. 'Collaboration' and 'solidarity' are terms that might be more helpful.

David Wilkinson
I like the term 'entrepreneur'. In a business context it speaks of someone who builds for the future, who sees new possibilities, who is prepared to take risks. I can see how some within the Church would react against it but there is creativity with entrepreneurship.

Ian Meredith
I run a business as well as being active in ministry (although I don't agree with the distinction). I am entrepreneurial in both.

Janet Sutton
Entrepreneur is not a term I would use in relation to my own pioneering ministry. I would prefer to use a word like prophetic. I suppose my own role is entrepreneurial as I began more or less with a blank piece of paper and a time span in which to achieve something. But it is not a definition that sits comfortably with me.

John Drane
I have no problem with the use of the word 'entrepreneur' in relation to ministry just so long as we don't imagine it excludes some people.

Jonny Baker
An entrepreneur is someone who builds something. And I like people who spot opportunities or gaps and are able to create something there.

It's an exciting word. For those of us who remember Margaret Thatcher it is also tainted with capitalist overtones but it's pretty clear that it's not being used in that way in the context of mission.

Robert Warren
Entrepreneurs are not often team players and can be driven rather than called. Servants and vocation are more important aspects of ministry that need exploring.

Ian Bell
I understand the reason why the term is used, but I struggle to feel entirely comfortable with it. It is difficult to detach the word 'entrepreneur' from the world of business and commerce – which has sufficient connotations of consumerism and materialism to make it somewhat unhelpful. Maybe 'spiritual entrepreneur' is slightly better?

The nine responses set out above are just a selection of those received, but they highlight the fact that the understanding of the term 'entrepreneur' in relation to Christian ministry is not straightforward. Although some of the respondents are content with the association, others express varying levels of concern and one respondent goes as far as stating 'I loathe the use of the term'. The responses to my survey were not subject to rigorous analysis, and in that sense I cannot claim that they are broadly representative of wider Christian attitudes. However, I strongly suggest that they point to the fact that in relation to Christian ministry the use of the term 'entrepreneur' is contested.

The warping power of Loadsamoney

In *The Enterprise Culture*, Peter Sedgwick acknowledges that 'There has been a suspicion of the market, wealth-creation and enterprise in the churches for a long time.'[4] This suspicion can be shaped by a number of factors, including gender, personality type, social class, family history, political affiliations, profession, personal experience of financial matters, church denomination and tradition, understanding of Scripture and image of God. I suggest, however, that a

---

[4] Peter Sedgwick, *The Enterprise Culture: A Challenging New Theology of Wealth Creation for the 1990s* (London: SPCK, 1992), 6.

further, external factor has contributed significantly to the negative perception of the entrepreneur articulated by some Christians. Mark Casson et al. refer to the period in the West, since the early 1980s, during which a particular image of the entrepreneur emerged in the public consciousness. And it is this image which continues to shape perceptions of entrepreneurs and entrepreneurial activity in the minds of many Christians who are uncomfortable with, or hostile to, the term. As Casson et al. write,

> The enterprise culture of the 1980s and 1990s was a natural reaction to some of the anti-entrepreneurial attitudes that had taken root in the West in the early post-war period. It should not be inferred, however, that this enterprise culture was based on a correct understanding of the role of the entrepreneur. The highly competitive and materialistic form of individualism promoted by 'enterprise culture' did not accurately represent the dominant values of successful entrepreneurs of previous generations.[5]

This observation is useful because it identifies a significant contribution to the negative associations that some make with the term 'entrepreneur'. An image of the entrepreneur as being responsible for, as well as a product of, a 'highly competitive and materialistic form of individualism'[6] is arguably dominant even today. One might say that, for some Christians, the entrepreneur has come to personify the morally suspect side of enterprise culture.

This negative image was caricatured and widely popularized in 1988 by the comedian Harry Enfield in his creation of the obnoxious character Loadsamoney, and – as one of the respondents to my survey pointed out – has been maintained by television programmes like *Dragons' Den* and *The Apprentice*. The image of the entrepreneur as obnoxious, self-seeking and motivated by money is still a key association for many Christians. In his interview response, for example, Jonny Baker recognizes that the term 'entrepreneur' continues to have negative associations with the culture of greed in the UK during the 1980s and early 1990s; with regard to the use of the term in relation to Christian ministry, Baker states that 'For those of us who remember Margaret Thatcher it is also tainted with capitalist overtones'.

---

[5] Mark Casson et al. (eds), *The Oxford Handbook of Entrepreneurship* (Oxford: Oxford University Press, 2006), 10.

[6] Casson et al., (eds) *Oxford Handbook*, 10.

However, Baker goes on to point out that 'it's pretty clear that it's not being used in that way in the context of mission'. Interestingly, having made their point about the enterprise culture of the 1980s and 1990s generating a wrong understanding of the role of the entrepreneur, Casson et al. go on to argue that the evidence 'suggests that successful entrepreneurship is as much a co-operative endeavour, mediated by social networks, as a purely individualistic and competitive one'.[7]

I suggest that Christians who respond hesitantly or negatively to language around entrepreneurship are likely to have less of an issue with entrepreneurship when it is conceived of as a co-operative, mutually supportive and non-competitive approach to life and work (and all that this implies for Christian ministry and mission) rather than as competitive, individualistic wealth creation. In an article on entrepreneurship published in the *Church of England Newspaper* I wrote, 'One minister, initially uncomfortable with the prospect of associating her ministry with that of being an entrepreneur, commented after a long discussion, "When I look at it like that, I'd like to be more entrepreneurial!"'[8]

I am not suggesting that conclusions can be drawn from this single example. However, I do propose that, by explaining the way in which I am using language with regard to entrepreneurship, I may be able to help Christians for whom the term has negative associations to understand how it could also be considered useful in reflecting on the potential shape of Christian ministry and mission today.

Entrepreneurs are not greedy

I have proposed that negative associations of the entrepreneur articulated by some Christians are, at least partially, a result of the image identified by Casson et al. as emerging from the enterprise culture. At the root of discomfort with this image for some Christians is a dual recognition that *greed* is a primary motivating factor for a good deal of wealth-generating activity and that greed (whether expressed individually or corporately) is inconsistent with Jesus' proclamation

---

[7] Casson et al. (eds), *Oxford Handbook*, 10.
[8] Published in 2012, <www.churchnewspaper.com/23985/archives/>.

of the coming kingdom of God.[9] It is possible to argue that this proclamation includes a 'preferential option for the poor'[10] and implies, therefore, a degree of hostility towards the creation, retention and use of wealth. Exponents of liberation theology,[11] for example, 'respond to the "reality" which confronts millions: poverty, appalling living conditions, malnutrition, inadequate health care, contrasting with the affluence [of the wealthy elites]'.[12] Those who cite Jesus' preferential option for the poor, including those who embrace theologies of liberation, point to the identity of those with whom Jesus chose to spend the majority of his time (the poor), the warnings he aimed at the rich and the explicit message of aspects of his teaching and a number of his parables.

In support of this view, particular examples from the Gospels might include Matthew who, at Jesus' call, abandons his toll-booth (Mark 2.14; Matthew 9.9; Luke 5.27–28), exchanging lucrative employment for a life on the road with a homeless rabbi.[13] One might also highlight the account of the rich young ruler (Matthew 19.16–30; Mark 10.17–31; Luke 18.18–25) to whom Jesus said, 'Go, sell everything you have and give to the poor, and you will have treasure in heaven. Then come, follow me' (Mark 10.21). There is the account of Zacchaeus, who upon encountering Jesus repents of his corrupt and self-seeking existence, returns four times what he has taken from those he has cheated and gives half of his possessions to the poor (Luke 19.1–10). Luke also records Jesus telling his hearers to 'Sell your possessions and give to the poor' (12.33). In Matthew's account of the Sermon on the Mount Jesus tells his hearers, 'Do not store up for yourself treasures on earth . . . But store up for yourselves

---

9   There is extensive literature dealing with Jesus' proclamation of the kingdom of God. Much of this is surveyed by George E. Ladd in *A Theology of the New Testament*, revised edn (Cambridge: The Lutterworth Press, 1994), and by N. T. Wright in *Jesus and the Victory of God* (London: SPCK, 2004). These two scholarly works discuss the significant contributions made by Schweitzer, Bultmann, Dodd, Jeremias, Cranfield, Allison, Beasley-Murray, Meyer and Dalman among others.

10 The Medellín Documents of the Conference of Latin American Bishops (1968), quoted in Joseph Milburn Thompson, *Introducing Catholic Social Thought* (New York: Orbis Books, 2010), 31.

11 For an introduction to liberation theology see Gustavo Gutiérrez, *A Theology of Liberation*, new edn (London: SCM Press, 2001), and Leonardo Boff and Clodovis Boff, *Introducing Liberation Theology* (New York: Orbis Books, 1996).

12 Christopher Rowland (ed.), *The Cambridge Companion to Liberation Theology* (Cambridge: Cambridge University Press, 1999), 5.

13 See Wright, *Jesus and the Victory of God*, 297–301.

treasures in heaven . . . You cannot serve both God and Money'
(Matthew 6.19–21, 24). We might also note Jesus' parable of the rich
fool (Luke 12.16–21) who resolves to build bigger barns in which to
store his surplus, but from whom God demands his life and about
whom Jesus says (v. 21), 'This is how it will be with whoever stores up
things for themselves but is not rich towards God.'

It is possible to see from these examples how one might argue that
Jesus' agenda was firmly anti-wealth and its creation and that following him meant becoming *like* the poor: turning one's back on worldly
wealth and time spent in its acquisition and embracing instead a life
of austerity, if not outright poverty.

On the other hand there are plenty of examples of Jesus spending
time with wealthy people who nevertheless expressed solidarity with
his message. The aforementioned Zacchaeus, described by Luke (19.2)
as wealthy, gave away half of his possessions, while Jesus announced
about him, 'Today salvation has come to this house' (Luke 19.9). But
Zacchaeus appeared to continue living in his home with the remain-
ing half of his possessions and to pursue his occupation as a chief
tax collector. Luke also reports that as Jesus travelled with his disciples from village to village proclaiming the kingdom, a large number
of women, including the wife of the manager of Herod's household,
'were helping to support them out of their own means' (Luke 8.1–3).
Joseph of Arimathea is described as a rich man (Matthew 27.57) who
is also a disciple of Jesus (John 19.38), and indeed he buries Jesus in
his own tomb (Matthew 27.57–60; Mark 15.43–46; Luke 23.50–53;
John 19.38–41). In relation to the examples provided about Jesus'
attitude to wealth and its creation and use by those around him, Tom
Wright argues that it is possible to detect in Jesus' call to his followers
different levels of challenge in relation to what must be abandoned
and what might be retained:

> It is clear that, while Jesus was perfectly content for some (like Mary
> and Martha) to remain loyal to him at a distance, he challenged some
> others to sell up and join him on the road. Some appear to have been
> with him from time to time; others to have provided for him and his
> disciples from their private property, which assumes that they still had
> property from which to gain income.[14]

---

[14] Wright, *Jesus and the Victory of God*, 298.

We should therefore proceed cautiously when attempting to explain Jesus' attitude to the creation and use of wealth. From what the Gospel writers report of Jesus, we gain the impression that his teaching was not concerned so much with opposition to making money in business, or with the fact of personal wealth, as with the *greed* that all too often lay behind these things. As noted above, Jesus' contemporary followers and supporters included those who had personal wealth or whose lives involved them in trade and commerce. Jesus told parables in which merchants and landowners[15] were not the focus of disapproval but players in a wider drama.

The central point here is that it is greed, and not wealth or its generation, that is inconsistent with Jesus' proclamation of the coming kingdom of God (Matthew 23.25; Mark 7.22; Luke 11.39; 12.15). Jesus inaugurates the kingdom and announces the inevitability of all things, including the creation and use of wealth, being brought under God's sovereign rule (Matthew 4.17; Mark 1.15) and in line, therefore, with principles of justice and provision for all.[16] This is part of the Good News announced by Jesus (Matthew 11.5; Luke 4.18): an end to an unfair system in which abundance for the powerful few was achieved at the cost of scarcity for the powerless majority.[17] So although we may argue that Jesus had no particular issue with business and the creation and use of wealth, his understanding of the nature and shape of the coming kingdom of God led him to say some very significant things about the *place* that wealth and its generation occupied in the heart and life of the individual.[18]

For twenty-first-century Christians, Jesus' proclamation of the coming kingdom of God continues to imply consequences for every sphere of human life and work, including business. His teaching and example, echoing the Jewish Law and the Prophets, include warnings about the creation of wealth for its own sake (Luke 12.13–21), since at the heart of this lies greed, which is a form of idolatry (Exodus 20.3, 23) and which points to a disregard for the needs of others. Both greed and a disregard for fellow human beings are outward signs of an attitude of the heart contrary to that

---

[15] Examples include Matthew 13.45–46; Mark 12.1–12; Luke 15.11–32; 16.1–13.
[16] See Leviticus 25.
[17] See N. T. Wright, *The New Testament and the People of God* (London: SPCK, 1992).
[18] See Wright, *Jesus and the Victory of God*, 302–3.

demanded by Jesus' summary of the Law (Matthew 22.37–40; Mark 12.29–31), and are therefore inconsistent with the values of the coming kingdom of God.

The purpose of this brief discussion has been to highlight the fact that where the creation of wealth is motivated by greed (whether individual or corporate), this is in direct conflict with Jesus' proclamation of the coming kingdom of God. The suspicion of the term 'entrepreneur' articulated by some Christians may therefore be rooted in a perception, generated by the enterprise culture of the 1980s and 1990s, that what motivates wealth-generating entrepreneurial activity is greed. For such Christians, greed indicates a disregard for God and for others, both of which are inconsistent with Jesus' teaching about the coming kingdom of God.

In relation to this point, however, we must keep in view the contention that, when we consider the role of entrepreneurs elsewhere in Western history, the understanding of the entrepreneur that emerged in enterprise culture was in fact a misunderstanding. It is also important to note that despite the resultant negative image of the entrepreneur for some Christians even today, research suggests that for many successful entrepreneurs, generation of wealth is a natural by-product of entrepreneurial activity rather than a primary motivating factor. In commenting on the work of the famous economist Joseph Schumpeter, sociologist Richard Swedberg says that, according to Schumpeter, 'It should be pointed out that money *per se* is not what ultimately motivates the entrepreneur'.[19] Schumpeter argued that the entrepreneur is driven by 'the desire for power and independence', 'the will to succeed' and 'the satisfaction of getting things done'.[20] According to a number of significant studies, becoming involved in entrepreneurial activity because it is interesting and enjoyable is a key motivating factor for many entrepreneurs,[21] as is a

---

[19] Richard Swedberg (ed.), *Entrepreneurship: The Social Science View* (Oxford: Oxford University Press, 2000), 16.

[20] Swedberg, *Entrepreneurship*, 16.

[21] See Frederic Delmar and Frederic C. Witte, 'The Psychology of the Entrepreneur', in Sarah Carter and Dylan Jones-Evans (eds), *Enterprise and Small Business: Principles, Practice and Policy* (Harlow: Prentice Hall, 2000); Teresa M. Amabile, 'Motivating Creativity in Organisations: On Doing What You Love and Loving What You Do', *California Management Review* 40:1 (1997), 39–58.

high need for achievement[22] and a desire for autonomy.[23] In relation to this last point, David Kirby echoes Schumpeter's view in stating that 'desire to manage or take ownership of one's own life is a central feature of entrepreneurship'.[24]

To sum up, in advocating a deliberate use of the term 'entrepreneur' in relation to Christian ministry, it is important to note the suspicions and negative associations that some Christians might have and to remain alert to the contested nature of the word. However, this book is rooted in the belief that the term has much to offer the Church: when we move the focus away from wealth creation and place it instead on a range of visionary and creative qualities that entrepreneurs exhibit, we will come to see that when these are exercised by Christians in a receptive context, they are capable of producing valuable outcomes both in the Church and the wider community.

The trouble with a definition . . .

It is important, however, to acknowledge that there is no agreed definition of the entrepreneur, either in social science literature or in common use. Peter Drucker goes as far as saying that there is 'total confusion over the terms entrepreneur and entrepreneurship',[25] while Brockhaus points out that 'the literature appears to support the argument that there is no generic definition of the entrepreneur'.[26] Kuratko and Hodgetts highlight the fact that 'no single definition of "entrepreneur" exists and no one profile can represent today's entrepreneur'.[27] Ricketts follows this, explaining that 'Entrepreneurship is not a concept that has a tightly agreed definition.'[28] Licht and Siegel also acknowledge the lack of an agreed definition for entrepreneurship and ask, with an economic focus uppermost in their minds, 'for

---

[22] David C. McClelland, *The Achieving Society* (Princeton, NJ: Van Nostrand, 1961).

[23] See Sally Caird, 'The Enterprising Tendency of Occupational Groups' *International Small Business Journal* 9: 4 (1991), 75–81; McClelland, *Achieving Society*.

[24] David A. Kirby, *Entrepreneurship* (Maidenhead: McGraw-Hill Education, 2003), 113.

[25] Peter F. Drucker, *Innovation and Entrepreneurship* (Oxford: Elsevier, 1985), 19.

[26] Robert H. Brockhaus, 'Foreword', in Robert H. Brockhaus et al. (eds), *Entrepreneurship Education: A Global View* (Aldershot: Ashgate Publishing, 2001), ix.

[27] Donald F. Kuratko and Richard M. Hodgetts, *Entrepreneurship: A Contemporary Approach*, 5th edn (Sydney: Harcourt College Publishers, 2001), 28.

[28] Martin Ricketts, 'Theories of Entrepreneurship: Historical Development and Critical Assessment', in Casson et al., *Oxford Handbook*, 34.

example, whether innovation is a necessary element or does self-employment suffice, or whether self-employment and ownership of a small business firm are equally entrepreneurial'.[29] They highlight the fact that the lack of '[a widely] agreed definition makes it difficult to compare and even relate studies to one another'.[30] In the introduction to their work on the entrepreneurial personality, Chell et al. also highlight the absence of a 'standard, universally accepted definition of entrepreneurship';[31] they quote Livesay, who suggests that 'successful entrepreneurship is an art form as much as, or perhaps more than, it is an economic activity, and as such is as difficult as any other artistic activity to explain in terms of origin, method or environmental influence'.[32]

Chell et al. ponder whether it is futile to persist in asking questions about *what* entrepreneurship is and *who* entrepreneurs are. And, to emphasize the point, they draw on Kilby's likening of the search for the entrepreneur to hunting the Heffalump. Kilby writes,

> [The Heffalump] is a rather large and very important animal. He has been hunted by many individuals using various ingenious trapping devices, but no one so far has succeeded in capturing him. All who claim to have caught sight of him report that he is enormous, but they disagree on his particularities.[33]

And it is here that an issue especially pertinent to this book comes into focus. The term 'entrepreneur' means different things to different people. The term itself is relatively young and the nature of the activity to which it pertains has evolved, and continues to do so, over time and across cultures. It is widely used in large and small business, in industry, in politics, in the media and entertainment industries, and increasingly in the not-for-profit sector. It continues to be studied by academics working across the social sciences in a variety of disciplines

---

[29] Amir N. Licht and Jordan I. Siegel, 'The Social Dimensions of Entrepreneurship', in Casson et al., *Oxford Handbook*, 512.

[30] Licht and Siegal, in Casson et al., *Oxford Handbook*, 512.

[31] Elizabeth Chell et al., *The Entrepreneurial Personality: Concepts, Cases and Categories* (London: Routledge, 1991), 1.

[32] Harold C. Livesay, 'Entrepreneurial Histroy', in Calvin C. Kent, Donald L. Sexton and Karl H. Vesper (eds), *Encyclopedia of Entrepreneurship* (Englewood Cliffs, NJ: Prentice-Hall, 1982), quoted in Chell et al., *Entrepreneurial Personality*, 11.

[33] Peter M. Kilby (ed.), *Entrepreneurship and Economic Development* (New York: Macmillan, 1971), quoted in Chell et al., *Entrepreneurial Personality*, 2.

including economics, psychology, sociology, anthropology[34] and practical theology. Given the widespread recognition that there is no agreed definition of entrepreneur or entrepreneurship, and the diversity of situations within which these words are in use, it seems that no authoritative, widely agreed definition of the entrepreneur exists, or indeed will ever be possible.

However, as we shall see, this does not mean the term is unusable or that we cannot put forward a definition that is in sympathy with a mainstream understanding of it. As I noted in my introduction, it was the lack of an agreed definition of the entrepreneur that led me to construct my own for use in the context of Christian ministry and mission.

Origin and evolution of the term 'entrepreneur'

A recognizably modern idea of the entrepreneur began to emerge in Europe, England and the United States in the eighteenth and nineteenth centuries.[35] The origin of the word provides us with some helpful insights into the development of the concept. Entrepreneur derives from the French words *entre*, meaning 'between', and *prendre*, which is the verb 'to take'. The French verb *entreprendre* means 'to undertake' or 'to do something'.[36] Bolton and Thompson suggest that these origins might imply that entrepreneur 'was another name for a merchant who acts as a go-between for parties in the trading process'.[37] Swedberg draws on the work of economist Bert Hoselitz to argue that the verb 'was originally used in the Middle Ages in the sense of "a person who is active, who gets things done".[38]

For Bolton and Thompson the origin of the term is an important indicator of what the entrepreneur does and achieves.[39] They argue that, although the term itself may not have emerged until

---

[34] For a survey of the social science literature, see Swedberg, *Entrepreneurship*.

[35] See Sydney G. Checkland, *The Rise of Industrial Society in England 1815–1885* (London: Longmans, Green & Co., 1964).

[36] Swedberg, *Entrepreneurship*, 11.

[37] Bill Bolton and John Thompson, *Entrepreneurs: Talent, Temperament, Technique*, 2nd edn (Oxford: Elsevier, 2004), 14.

[38] Bert Hoselitz, 'The Early History of Entrepreneurial Theory: Explorations in Entrepreneurial History 3' (1951), 193–220, in Swedberg, *Entrepreneurship*, 11.

[39] Bolton and Thompson, *Entrepreneurs*, 14.

the eighteenth century, it is possible to identify the entrepreneur throughout history. Drawing on the French verb *entreprendre*, they explain that this relates to undertaking a venture 'but it can also be used in relation to starting a new venture, and this is central to the use of the word "entrepreneur" in English'.[40]

In Bolton and Thompson's view it is possible to identify figures throughout history – including figures in Scripture – as entrepreneurs, because the process of entrepreneurship is not shackled to the emergence of the word in eighteenth-century France or the subsequent evolution of the concept in economic theory.[41] Casson et al. assert that 'the term "entrepreneur" appears to have been introduced into economic theory by Richard Cantillon (1759), an Irish economist of French descent'.[42] In his theory of the entrepreneur, presented in a work entitled *Essay on the Nature of Commerce in General* (*c.* 1730), Cantillon 'stresses function, rather than personality or social status'.[43] 'According to Cantillon, the entrepreneur is a specialist in taking risk.'[44] This notion is consistent with Bolton and Thompson's association of the word with a merchant acting as go-between for trading parties; an undertaking that would almost certainly involve personal financial risk.

Drawing on Hebert and Link,[45] Monica Lindh de Montoya writes that 'Cantillon's entrepreneur is someone who engages in exchanges for profit, using business judgement in a situation of uncertainty, buying at one price to sell at another, uncertain price in the future.'[46] Cantillon's entrepreneur

> insures workers by buying their output for resale before consumers have indicated how much they are willing to pay for it. The workers receive an assured income, while the entrepreneur bears the risk caused by price fluctuations in consumer markets.[47]

[40] Bolton and Thompson, *Entrepreneurs*, 15.

[41] Bolton and Thompson, *Entrepreneurs*, 14–16.

[42] Casson et al., *Oxford Handbook*, 3.

[43] Monica Lindh de Montoya, 'Entrepreneurship and Culture: The Case of Freddy, the Strawberry Man', in Swedberg, *Entrepreneurship*, 338.

[44] Casson et al., *Oxford Handbook*, 3.

[45] Robert F. Hebert and Albert N. Link, *The Entrepreneur: Mainstream Views and Radical Critiques* (New York: Praeger, 1988).

[46] De Montoya, 'Entrepreneurship and Culture', in Swedberg, *Entrepreneurship*, 338.

[47] Casson et al., *Oxford Handbook*, 3.

De Montoya tells us that as well as highlighting the bearing of risk as a function of the entrepreneur, Cantillon also identified

> business judgement, or decision-making as important to entrepreneurship; a theme echoed by Marshall (1925), Mises (1951) and Schultz (1980) among others such as Kirzner (1985) who writes of the entrepreneur as someone who discovers profit opportunities and is an allocator of resources among alternative possible uses.[48]

This identification of the entrepreneur with judgement and decision-making is picked up by Casson et al., who argue that the insights of economists over more than two hundred years – such as Cantillon (1755), Marshall (1919), Knight (1921), Schumpeter (1934), von Hayek (1937) and Kirzner (1973) – 'can be synthesized by identifying an entrepreneurial function that is common to all approaches. This is the exercise of judgement in decision making'.[49]

John Stuart Mill is credited with introducing the term into English economics in the mid-nineteenth century.[50] In his writing, Mill highlights an important distinction between the entrepreneur (or undertaker, i.e. one who undertakes) and the manager; he states that the profit from an undertaking engaged in by an entrepreneur had to be sufficient to provide 'a sufficient equivalent for abstinence, indemnity for risk, and remuneration for the labour and skill required for superintendence. While the difference between the interest and the gross profit remunerates the exertions and risks of the undertaker.'[51]

Mill's use of the phrase 'indemnity for risk' is highly significant and is likely to have influenced his choice of the word 'undertaker' rather than manager when outlining the function of the entrepreneur. Although Cantillon is credited as being the first to identify the bearing of risk as a key function or specialism of the entrepreneur, in Mill's writing we have the first association *in English* of the entrepreneur with the notion of risk bearing. It is an association which continues to the present day – though it has been contested by some,

---

[48] De Montoya, 'Entrepreneurship and Culture', in Swedberg, *Entrepreneurship*, 338.

[49] Casson et al., *Oxford Handbook*, 3.

[50] Joseph A. Schumpeter, *History of Economic Analysis* (London: George Allen and Unwin, 1954), 556.

[51] John Stuart Mill, *Principles of Political Economy: The People's Edition* (London: Longmans, Green & Co., 1898), 245–6.

the most prominent of whom is Joseph A. Schumpeter,[52] for whom 'the supply of capital and the supply of entrepreneurial services were quite distinct, and risk attached to the former not the latter'.[53]

In his book, *Risk, Uncertainty and Profit*,[54] the US economist Frank Knight developed Cantillon's ideas and 'distinguished between risk, which is insurable, and uncertainty, which is not'.[55] According to Knight, 'Risk refers to recurrent events whose relative frequency is known from past experience, while uncertainty relates to unique events whose probability can only be subjectively estimated.'[56] In Knight's opinion, the majority of risks relating to production and marketing fell into the second category, uncertainty. The owners of businesses cannot insure against such risks, argued Knight, which meant that they themselves were left to bear them. Casson et al. report that for Knight 'Pure profit is the reward for bearing this uninsurable risk: it is the reward of the entrepreneur.'[57]

The writing of Joseph A. Schumpeter has arguably made the biggest contribution to popular notions of entrepreneurship. According to Casson et al., Schumpeter was 'concerned with the "high level" kind of entrepreneurship that, historically, has led to the creation of railways, the development of the chemical industry, and the growth of integrated oil companies'.[58] He viewed the entrepreneur as a revolutionary innovator who, in creating new industries, participated in major structural changes in the economy. He emphasized the importance of the entrepreneur in national economic development, and he is responsible for the metaphor 'gale of creative destruction'[59] which describes the 'competitive processes of capitalist development'.[60] The 'unceasing gale derives from the energy of entrepreneurs'.[61]

---

[52] See Joseph A. Schumpeter, *The Theory of Economic Development* (Harvard: Harvard University Press, 1911).

[53] Martin Ricketts, 'The Entrepreneur in Classical Political Economy', in Casson et al., *Oxford Handbook*, 41.

[54] Frank H. Knight, *Risk, Uncertainty and Profit* (Boston: Houghton Mifflin, 1921).

[55] Casson et al., *Oxford Handbook*, 3.

[56] Casson et al., *Oxford Handbook*, 3.

[57] Casson et al., *Oxford Handbook*, 3.

[58] Casson et al., *Oxford Handbook*, 3.

[59] Joseph A. Schumpeter, *Capitalism, Socialism, and Democracy* (New York: Harper & Brothers, 1942), 132.

[60] Ricketts, in Casson et al., *Oxford Handbook*, 46.

[61] Ricketts, in Casson et al., *Oxford Handbook*, 46.

Ricketts tells us that for Schumpeter, entrepreneurship is 'the force that prevents the economic system running down and continually resists the approach of the classic stationary state'.[62] This notion is particularly interesting when transferred to the context of the Church, where one might argue that the presence and activity of entrepreneurial ministers are a force that prevent denominations and, indeed, individual churches, from 'running down' and becoming stationary.

Schumpeter's theory of the entrepreneur is perhaps most fully articulated in the second chapter ('Entrepreneurship as Innovation') of *The Theory of Economic Development*.[63] It is here that Schumpeter

> says that entrepreneurship can be defined as the making of a '*new combination*' of already existing materials and forces; that entrepreneurship consists of making innovations, as opposed to inventions; and that no one is an entrepreneur for ever, only when he or she is actually doing the innovative activity.[64]

The emphasis here is on function: what the entrepreneur *does*. We might say that for Schumpeter particular individuals engage in necessary entrepreneurial activity from time to time.

Schumpeter's emphasis on discontinuous activity, however, differs from that of Bolton and Thompson. They tie identity and function together and associate the entrepreneur's ability to innovate with habit. For Bolton and Thompson, the entrepreneur *habitually* engages in creative innovation in order to 'build something of recognized value'.[65] Whereas Schumpeter focused on the entrepreneur as a person with 'the vision and willpower to "found a private kingdom"'[66] and who performed a vital economic function by engaging in 'revolutionary and discontinuous'[67] innovation, Bolton and Thompson's entrepreneur 'just cannot stop being an entrepreneur'.[68] He or she is likely to be found in any number of contexts beyond the world of business and commerce – including the Church!

---

[62] Ricketts, in Casson et al., *Oxford Handbook*, 46.
[63] Swedberg reviews Schumpeter's contribution to economic thought with particular attention to his theory of entrepreneurship which, Swedberg points out, 'is part of an attempt to construct a whole new type of economic theory'. Swedberg, *Entrepreneurship*, 12.
[64] Swedberg, *Entrepreneurship*, 15.
[65] Bolton and Thompson, *Entrepreneurs*, 16.
[66] Ricketts, in Casson et al., *Oxford Handbook*, 46.
[67] Ricketts, in Casson et al., *Oxford Handbook*, 46.
[68] Bolton and Thompson, *Entrepreneurs*, 16.

2

Definitions of the entrepreneur

In the Introduction to this book I proposed my own definition of the entrepreneur. I shall open this chapter by spending a little more time with that definition before moving on to consider an alternative definition suggested by Bill Bolton and John Thompson. Their work on entrepreneurship has been used widely, especially in churches, and because of this it formed a significant backdrop to my own research and will be useful to us here.

It may seem odd to put forward my own definition and then spend time explaining someone else's. But, as I have pointed out, there are a plethora of definitions in use, because the term 'entrepreneur' means different things to different people. In order for you, the reader, to gain a useful understanding of who the entrepreneurs in our midst are and what they might do, it is important to consider more than one definition. By looking at an example in addition to my own, I hope that a richer and more nuanced understanding of the entrepreneur will begin to emerge. By the end of the chapter you should have a clearer understanding both of the way in which I am proposing to use the term in relation to Christian ministry, and of who the entrepreneurs might be in your own community. I also hope that reading this chapter results in a growing sense of enthusiasm as you imagine the possibilities that could open up in your own situation if an entrepreneurial approach to ministry and mission were encouraged and supported.

A little more on my own definition . . .

In the Introduction I set out the following definition of the entrepreneur:

A visionary who, in partnership with God and others, challenges the status quo by energetically creating and innovating in order to shape something of kingdom value.

When I first began to research entrepreneurship I found scores of definitions in the literature. My own effort was an attempt to propose an understanding that would enable entrepreneurial ministry to be discussed constructively in the context of the Church. In the Introduction to this book I provided a brief explanation of the components of my definition, suggesting that visionaries are those who see what *might* be as well as what *is*, and that through acting wisely, building trust and communicating effectively, they share this vision and collaborate with others to see it realized. I pointed out that entrepreneurs have energy that translates into making things happen and that this energy is often directed at moving beyond the status quo, or the apparent limits of the way things are. I recognized that this can make them quite annoying to the rest of us but I explained that for Christians, Jesus provides an example of someone who was prepared to disturb individuals and institutions where apathy and the love of comfort had crept in. I suggested that reflecting on Jesus' entrepreneurial approach to ministry might help us to recognize and celebrate the gift of entrepreneurship in our Christian communities.

The three aspects of my definition that I didn't enlarge upon in the Introduction were 'creating', 'innovating' and 'in order to shape something of kingdom value'. Entrepreneurs are creative in the sense that they are able to make connections that the rest of us cannot or do not. They have the ability to recognize previously unrelated elements that might be brought into a relationship in order to open up fresh potential or new possibilities. Being creative doesn't mean that entrepreneurs are gifted artists but rather that they have a way of looking at the world that often produces fresh insights.

If creativity is about spotting potential connections, innovation is about making those connections a reality. Innovation may begin with creativity but it must move beyond insights and ideas to take what is already in existence and develop it so that it has an improved or entirely new application. Entrepreneurs, then, are individuals who not only spot new or refreshed potential in people, places and things, but also take action to see that potential realized.

In my working definition entrepreneurs in ministry act in this way in order to shape something of kingdom value. I've used the word 'shape' here because, although entrepreneurs in the Church might well start something from scratch, this is not always the case. It is more likely that they will take something that is already in existence – a service, community gathering or outreach initiative – and, by creating and innovating alongside others, *shape* a refreshed version that is more fruitful or less time-consuming than the previous version or is simply better suited to the requirements of those involved.

Entrepreneurs in ministry do what they do because they are following Jesus Christ and seeking to make a difference for him in the world. The fruit of their efforts will be faithful and multifaceted witness to Jesus. In this sense, then, they are shaping something of kingdom value rather than keeping busy or building an empire. To the extent that entrepreneurial ministers strive to contribute to the work of God in the world, their efforts have the potential to be of kingdom value. Or they should do!

Of course, not all entrepreneurial ministers will get it right all of the time. To some extent mistakes, mixed motives, disappointment, disagreement and unsuccessful projects are bound to be a part of the mix. But in the grace of God none of these things needs to be unredeemable. And, as entrepreneurial ministers apply themselves to learning to grow in love, humility and wisdom, mistakes and mess can become opportunities for learning and growth.

I have already pointed out that entrepreneurs can be annoying. None of us really enjoys change and we are often especially irritated when the possibility of the new or different is brought to our attention by someone with apparently boundless energy whose glass is always half full. However, since, as the Church, we are going about God's work and not our own, the result of ignoring or opposing the entrepreneurs in our midst will not be a quiet life in which we are simply able to rest content in enjoying the various good things handed to us by previous generations. Ignoring or opposing the contribution of entrepreneurs is likely to result in stagnation, unfaithfulness to our first love (Jesus) and ineffectiveness in joining in with God's work in the world. Entrepreneurs are a gift of God to the Church and they are placed among us to help us avoid unfaithfulness, ineffectiveness, stagnation and the gradual slide into introversion and irrelevance.

Bolton and Thompson's definition

During my research I paid particular attention to the work of Bill Bolton and John Thompson. Bolton and Thompson's online tool for assessing entrepreneurial potential has been used by the Church of England as part of the selection process for Ordained Pioneer Ministers (OPMs).[1] Their book, *Entrepreneurs: Talent, Temperament, Technique*,[2] contains a definition of the entrepreneur that I considered in some detail as I developed my own working definition. Their definition is given below in the context of a brief summary of the aims of their book. Following this I consider each component of their definition in greater depth, drawing also on the work of an American writer on entrepreneurship and the church, Michael Simms.

Entrepreneurs: Talent, Temperament, Technique

In *Entrepreneurs: Talent, Temperament, Technique*, Bolton and Thompson set out their understanding of the entrepreneur. In light of the discussion at the start of the previous chapter on the contested nature of the term 'entrepreneur', Bolton and Thompson's comments about the hoped-for outcomes from their book are interesting:

> We hope that it [the book] will make you think differently about entrepreneurs and understand that not all of them are out there making money at other people's expense. We would like to redeem the word 'entrepreneur' and give it a more positive image linking it with concepts such as integrity and philanthropy. Our emphasis on entrepreneurial talent, as being something a person is given, promotes that end.[3]

They go on to remark that 'We want entrepreneurs to become both socially acceptable and academically respectable. Only when this happens will the culture barriers in society come down.'[4]

---

[1] Bolton and Thompson's First Stage Entrepreneur Indicator (FSEI) can be accessed at <www.efacets.co.uk>. Their work on entrepreneurship has also been used by the Anglican dioceses of Chelmsford and Southwell.

[2] Bill Bolton and John Thompson, *Entrepreneurs: Talent, Temperament, Technique*, 2nd edn (Oxford: Elsevier, 2004).

[3] Bolton and Thompson, *Entrepreneurs*, 5.

[4] Bolton and Thompson, *Entrepreneurs*, 5.

Other outcomes that Bolton and Thompson hope will result from their exploration of what entrepreneurs do include a desire that various financial and bureaucratic hurdles to entrepreneurship are removed; that those with the potential to be entrepreneurs are given opportunities; and that those who work in large organizations become more enterprising. The attention that Bolton and Thompson pay to entrepreneurial behaviour in a diverse range of situations is one of the factors that makes their understanding of the entrepreneur particularly helpful in the context of this book. Among the most significant of their hopes is that the role that 'clusters of entrepreneurs can play in economic and social development [is] recognized'.[5] They argue that

> A few entrepreneurs can make a difference but when there are many of them and their number reaches a critical mass, a region or community simply takes off. Economic growth and social development become self-sustaining and an entrepreneurial culture develops.[6]

Their examples of this include the Renaissance, the Industrial Revolution and the current high-technology revolution, typified by the Silicon Valley phenomenon. While noting the argument that those with real entrepreneurial flair will simply get on with it regardless of whether they are alone and in spite of the difficulties involved, however, they also explain that they do not subscribe to the 'macho view of entrepreneurship'[7] and point out that when the environment is not receptive to entrepreneurs 'there will be significantly fewer of them and it is the number of entrepreneurs that is the critical factor'.[8]

Bolton and Thompson observe that entrepreneurs do not fit a particular *type*. Significantly, they also contend that 'our education system and our professions – to name but two factors – not only inhibit the flowering of entrepreneurial talent, they positively discourage it'.[9] Although there is insufficient space in this book to explore the impact on entrepreneurial ministers of theological training and the move towards professionalization, this last point is pertinent; given that this book has partially emerged from my

---

[5] Bolton and Thompson, *Entrepreneurs*, 6.
[6] Bolton and Thompson, *Entrepreneurs*, 6.
[7] Bolton and Thompson, *Entrepreneurs*, 6.
[8] Bolton and Thompson, *Entrepreneurs*, 6.
[9] Bolton and Thompson, *Entrepreneurs*, 14.

work as a theological educator, it provokes reflection on the pedagogy underpinning and informing not only my own professional practice but also the selection processes and training institutions of all Christian denominations.

Having argued that the 'who' question in relation to entrepreneurs is difficult, Bolton and Thompson go on to state that the 'what' is easier. This is because the answer is based on what the entrepreneur does (the process) or achieves (the results). In constructing their definition of the entrepreneur, Bolton and Thompson 'see the "who" as a person and the "what" as a process that is habitual and involves creativity and innovation and results in something of value that can be recognised by others'.[10] They go on to remark that 'The building process, of course, first needs an opportunity to build on and this is something the entrepreneur is always able to spot.'[11]

Growing out of these observations, Bolton and Thompson's definition of the entrepreneur is

> A person who habitually creates and innovates to build something of recognized value around perceived opportunities.[12]

You will note that there is both some similarity to my definition and some rather different emphases. Because of my concern with the activity of entrepreneurs in the context of Christian ministry and mission, my own definition makes specific mention of the kingdom of God. In contrast, as their concern was to construct a definition that would be applicable across a wide range of situations in which entrepreneurs are active, Bolton and Thompson do not mention this. In the rest of this chapter I shall discuss each element of Bolton and Thompson's definition in turn.

'A person'

Bolton and Thompson explain that in opening their definition with 'a person', their aim is to emphasize the involvement of personality rather than a system. They add that 'a person' can be a group of people, since 'it is possible to describe teams and even organizations

---

[10] Bolton and Thompson, *Entrepreneurs*, 16.

[11] Bolton and Thompson, *Entrepreneurs*, 16.

[12] Bolton and Thompson, *Entrepreneurs*, 16.

as entrepreneurial.[13] In this, they echo Schumpeter's later writing, in which he expressed the view that 'the entrepreneur does not have to be a single person but can equally well be an organization, either a political or an economic one. What matters is behaviour, not the actor.'[14]

In the context of the Church, entrepreneurial ministers will ideally find themselves operating as members of entrepreneurial teams within an entrepreneurial organization. In reality, though, entrepreneurial ministers are likely to be working alone and against the grain, since local congregations, as well as the denominations more generally, tend – like most large organizations – towards an inherent conservatism.

Entrepreneurial ministers will nevertheless find ways to satisfy their habitual entrepreneurial flair. At best, with grace and wisdom, this flair has the potential to be well directed and to gain and retain the support of the congregation, resulting in the creation of valuable outcomes. At worst, there is the risk that the entrepreneurial minister will be responsible for starting initiatives that the congregation are unwilling or unable to support, or that result in the minister being viewed by the institution as difficult, eccentric or otherwise problematic.

Kirby picks up on what is at the heart of the last point, stating that

> Enterprising individuals are often not attracted to large organizations and tend not to be found in them. When they are, either they become worn down by bureaucracy or they leave. Often, large organizations see such people as loners rather than team players, or as eccentrics more interested in pet projects than corporate objectives. They are frequently viewed as cynics, rebels, free spirits.[15]

The traditional denominations and the new arrivals alike are institutions, albeit of varying sizes, and it is possible to recognize Kirby's point in relation to both. It is also possible to make a challenging contrast between the radical life and teaching of Jesus Christ (and the example of the early Christians) and the Church as it developed into an institution through the ages and across the globe. Although this contrast is all too easily simplified, the tension between the radical and the institutional is an inherent part of the story of the Church

---

[13] Bolton and Thompson, *Entrepreneurs*, 16.

[14] Schumpeter, in Richard Swedberg (ed.), *Entrepreneurship: The Social Science View* (Oxford: Oxford University Press, 2000), 17.

[15] David A. Kirby, *Entrepreneurship* (Maidenhead: McGraw-Hill Education, 2003), 302.

and is something it continues to wrestle with. And the perception and treatment of entrepreneurial ministers by others–with some denominations being more naturally receptive to entrepreneurial qualities and others being resistant – is an aspect of that struggle.

It has become popular to use the terms 'organizational entrepreneurship', 'corporate entrepreneurship' and 'intrapreneurship' in describing the 'process in which innovative products or processes are developed by creating an entrepreneurial culture within an organization.'[16] Although it is outside the scope of this book to consider whether our various churches are moving in this direction, we may note that entrepreneurial ministers cannot accurately be described as 'intrapreneurs' simply because they work for a large organization. According to Kirby, intrapreneurship is a deliberate and strategic approach by large organizations to 'integrate the strengths of the entrepreneurial small firm (creativity, flexibility, innovativeness, closeness to market, etc.) with the market power and financial resources of the large organization.'[17] Churches in the West have not adopted an explicitly intrapreneurial approach at any level and I suggest that those ministers who act entrepreneurially do so because it is in their nature to act in this way, not because the organization of which they are a part has made any deliberate effort to encourage this type of activity.

It might be helpful to point out that while intrapreneurship and entrepreneurship share characteristics such as a focus on innovation, the creation of value-added products and an involvement in 'risky' activities, there are significant differences. Kirby tells us that 'intrapreneurship is restorative while entrepreneurship is developmental',[18] and that it is 'intended to counter stagnation within the organization'.[19] He goes on to say that 'while the entrepreneur is concerned to overcome obstacles in the market, the intrapreneur has to overcome corporate obstacles'.[20] I would argue that the minister acting entrepreneurially has to overcome both!

While Bolton and Thompson state that 'a person' can be either an individual or a group of people, Michael Simms contends in *Faith Entrepreneurs* (2006) that being 'an agent of change who adds value

16 Kirby, *Entrepreneurship*, 300.
17 Kirby, *Entrepreneurship*, 300.
18 Kirby, *Entrepreneurship*, 300.
19 Kirby, *Entrepreneurship*, 300.
20 Kirby, *Entrepreneurship*, 300.

through creatively and passionately launching bold initiatives, all the while taking calculated risks *for God*[21] is never a solitary venture. Simms argues that, for those acting entrepreneurially 'for God', the key is to join with likeminded others whom he describes as 'gifted and passionate visionaries and implementers who help define our mission, help assess needs, analyse opportunities, and work together in meeting human needs and operating in our community'.[22] Although the lack of presence and availability of likeminded others may well be an issue for entrepreneurial ministers working in rural or socially challenging contexts, I suggest that ministers' understanding of their role should include actively seeking out and utilizing whatever others have to offer[23] as they endeavour to 'habitually create and innovate to build something of recognized value'.[24]

'Habitually'

Bolton and Thompson tell us that 'habit' is the characteristic that distinguishes entrepreneurs from owner-managers in business. They explain, as noted above, that 'the true entrepreneur just cannot stop being an entrepreneur'.[25] As illustration they quote entrepreneur Bo Peabody, who says, 'People ask me how to become an entrepreneur and I can't tell them. It's something innate. I couldn't stop even if I wanted to.'[26] Ucbasaran, Westhead and Wright support this point, commenting that the 'evidence generally suggests that habitual entrepreneurs are a widespread phenomenon'.[27]

For Simms, one of the ways in which faith entrepreneurs achieve change in the social sector is by 'recognizing and relentlessly pursuing

[21] Michael Keith Simms, *Faith Entrepreneurs: Empowering People by Faith, Nonprofit Organizational Leadership, and Entrepreneurship* (Lincoln, NE: iUniverse, 2006), 22–3.
[22] Simms, *Faith Entrepreneurs*, 23.
[23] Moynagh points out that 'entrepreneurship is a team process', and explains that it 'involves a variety of activities' and 'requires one or more teams rather than a single person'. He goes on to say that entrepreneurs 'contribute to the team in many different ways, depending on their capabilities and personal traits'. Michael Moynagh, *Church for Every Context: An Introduction to Theology and Practice* (London: SCM Press, 2012), 230.
[24] Bolton and Thompson, *Entrepreneurs*, 16.
[25] Bolton and Thompson, *Entrepreneurs*, 16.
[26] Bolton and Thompson, *Entrepreneurs*, 16.
[27] Deniz Ucbasaran, Paul Westhead and Mike Wright, 'Habitual Entrepreneurs', in Mark Casson et al. (eds), *The Oxford Handbook of Entrepreneurship* (Oxford: Oxford University Press, 2006), 464.

new opportunities to serve that mission'.[28] Simms' word 'relent-less' seems to catch something of what Bolton and Thompson have in mind when they use the word 'habitual'. While 'relentless' argu-ably implies a less rhythmic or sustainable approach to activity than 'habitual', both words open up a hugely important theme in relation to those who engage in entrepreneurial activity, and that is consist-ency of involvement in entrepreneurial activities over time. For both Bolton and Thompson and for Simms, entrepreneurs *consistently* build things of recognized value. They start a project, or a number of projects, that are very likely linked together, and as each project reaches completion, they begin something new. One successful pro-ject leads to the next, or may even open up the opportunity for the next, and so it goes on.

Entrepreneurial ministers may experience less fertile seasons when, because of illness, family concerns or the sheer weight of other demands, entrepreneurial activity is ticking over or even temporar-ily placed on hold. But this will not be the normal state of affairs, and what marks the entrepreneurial minister out is that his or her 'normal' operating mode will involve the experience of being driven towards 'habitually creating and innovating to build something of recognized value'.[29]

'Creates'

Bolton and Thompson explain that the word 'creates' features in their definition in order to highlight that 'entrepreneurs start from scratch and bring something into being that was not there before'.[30] This notion is particularly significant in the context of this book since the concept of creativity has enormous theological relevance for Christians. Simms remarks that 'If we catch God's entrepreneurial vision . . . creativity and dreaming become the norm'.[31] Each Sunday Anglican clergy lead worship in which a confession of faith includes a statement of belief in a creator God.[32] Christians believe that in some

---

28 Simms, *Faith Entrepreneurs*, 25.
29 Bolton and Thompson, *Entrepreneurs*, 16.
30 Bolton and Thompson, *Entrepreneurs*, 16.
31 Simms, *Faith Entrepreneurs*, 21.
32 The Nicene Creed and the Apostles' Creed include references to God as 'maker' (Nicene) and 'creator' (Apostles').

sense human beings are created in the image of God (Genesis 1.27) and are therefore capable of expressing something of God's creativity in their own lives.[33]

In Bolton and Thompson's view this creativity is clearly in evidence in the entrepreneur and is an essential element in the process of entrepreneurship, while according to von Hayek, it is not just that the entrepreneur is creative and exercises creativity in the process of building something, but that 'new and unknown knowledge is being *created* through the process of entrepreneurship. To be an entrepreneur implies a "discovery process".'[34] De Montoya tells us that Kirzner also 'emphasized entrepreneurship as a creative act of discovery'.[35] These views dovetail well with the Christian understanding of discipleship as an continuing and relational process of discovery of God, of others, of self and of the nature of living as created beings, made in the image of a creator God, in a created world.[36]

Even in *The White Spider*, a classic work of mountaineering rather than economics, Heinrich Harrer writes of 'enterprising and daring men'[37] and their 'out-of-the-ordinary ideas',[38] and tells us that it is 'the eternal longing of every truly creative [person] to push on into unexplored country, to discover something entirely new'.[39] The sentiment communicated by Harrer's words seems to link with the nature of entrepreneurship that Bolton and Thompson outline and which I am exploring in relation to entrepreneurial ministers. The notion of 'enterprising and daring' *ministers* with 'out-of-the-ordinary ideas' and a creativity of spirit that continually provokes exploration into unexplored places and opportunities is a stimulating one. The research underpinning this book was motivated in part by a desire to engage with such ministers, to learn from them and to share knowledge

---

[33] For an exploration of this theme, see Dorothy L. Sayers, *The Mind of the Maker* (London: Continuum, 2004), and Oliver Davis, *The Creativity of God: World, Eucharist, Reason* (Cambridge: Cambridge University Press, 2004).

[34] Swedberg, *Entrepreneurship*, 20.

[35] Monica Lindh de Montoya, 'Entrepreneurship and Culture: The Case of Freddy, the Strawberry Man', in Swedberg, *Entrepreneurship*, 339.

[36] The use of 'creator' and 'created' in relation to God, the world and human beings, is to be distinguished from 'creationism'.

[37] Heinrich Harrer, *The White Spider: The Story of the North Face of the Eiger* (London: Harper Perennial, 2005), 30.

[38] Harrer, *White Spider*, 30.

[39] Harrer, *White Spider*, 29.

and insights with the wider Church in order that it might be better equipped to participate in the building of God's kingdom.

Duncan and colleagues nonetheless articulate a view that appears to be present to varying degrees in the western Church. Duncan writes: 'Creative people are, to be honest, a pain in the neck. They disrupt the established order by asking questions and experimenting with new ways of doing things when well-established procedures are available to provide direction.'[40] It is this negative view of the creativity demonstrated by entrepreneurs that leads to opposition to some of their initiatives, and overcoming such opposition is one of the challenges outlined in the following section.

'Innovates'

Bolton and Thompson include innovation in their definition, arguing that it differs from creativity in its importance to delivering the final application of the entrepreneurial venture. It is innovation, they argue, that ensures that the ideas generated by creativity become reality; entrepreneurs, they say, 'use their innovative talents to overcome obstacles that would stop most people. For them every problem is a new opportunity.'[41]

Simms echoes this, stating that 'Entrepreneurship is about seeing, sizing and seizing new opportunities. This means taking on challenges in new ways, acting boldly and taking risks whilst expecting results that change lives. Change stands at the heart of entrepreneurship.'[42] Simms anticipates obstacles and difficulties for the faith entrepreneur, arguing that 'to get new results it's necessary to challenge existing mindsets.'[43] Challenge of this kind is arguably the most difficult of territories to navigate, and is part of the experience of many entrepreneurial ministers. For, unless the entrepreneurial minister identifies projects or opportunities that are in line with the congregation's expectations, it is the hearts and minds of the members of the congregation that are likely to need changing before the process of building something of recognized value can begin. Simms goes on to state that

---

[40] W. Jack Duncan, Peter M. Ginter, Andrew C. Rucks and T. Douglas Jacobs, 'Intrapreneurship and the Reinvention of the Corporation', *Business Horizons* 31:3 (1988), 16–21.

[41] Bolton and Thompson, *Entrepreneurs*, 16.

[42] Simms, *Faith Entrepreneurs*, 22.

[43] Simms, *Faith Entrepreneurs*, 22.

Entrepreneurs introduce new rules and new conditions for living. They don't accept what everyone else sees as reality. They look for a new reality behind what is seen by others. They go deeper to discover the truth that sheds light on what is masquerading as truth. They probe and investigate and consider alternatives. They develop new initiatives to bring the truth and power of God's kingdom to bear on our temporal world.[44]

In this he outlines a role for the entrepreneur that is, one might argue, prophetic in its nature.[45] As well as working with those whose minds may need changing and who may need to be helped to see differently, Simms' entrepreneurs also have to overcome difficulties in terms of lack of resources or bureaucratic obstacles. To do this, Simms, in line with Bolton and Thompson, argues that entrepreneurs engage in a 'process of continuous innovation, adaptation, learning',[46] by 'acting boldly without being limited to resources currently in hand'.[47] Simms explains that the faith entrepreneur 'Sees needs and seeks new ways to meet those needs – with little regard for what has been tried or never attempted.'[48]

Simms' point resonates with my own experience of pioneering work as an entrepreneurial minister. I have certainly heard the mantras, 'We tried that once and it didn't work!' or, 'We don't do that sort of thing here!' In response I have helped to develop various strategies for shaping a culture in which ideas that were perceived to be out of kilter with a previous culture could be generated, discussed and absorbed enthusiastically and expectantly.[49]

Kirby points out that large organizations inherently have too many levels of approval and argues that 'Multiple levels of management tend to stultify innovation as each level has the potential to kill the project.'[50] My own denomination, the Church of England, doesn't quite have multiple levels of management and, in the sense that they

[44] Simms, *Faith Entrepreneurs*, 22.
[45] For treatment of the nature of 'prophetic ministry', see Walter Brueggemann, *The Prophetic Imagination*, 2nd edn (Minneapolis, MN: Augsburg Fortress, 2001).
[46] Simms, *Faith Entrepreneurs*, 25.
[47] Simms, *Faith Entrepreneurs*, 25.
[48] Simms, *Faith Entrepreneurs*, 20.
[49] For an account of one aspect of my pioneering work as an entrepreneurial minister, see Michael Volland, *Through the Pilgrim Door: Pioneering a Fresh Expression of Church* (Eastbourne: Survivor, 2009).
[50] Kirby, *Entrepreneurship*, 301.

are not 'managed', the majority of parish priests operate with a fair degree of autonomy. However, most entrepreneurial ministers within the larger denominations who seek to build something of recognized value will clearly need to gain the support of colleagues and perhaps senior staff. Here, Kirby's point about the potential death of projects at the hands of various levels of management has some relevance. It is outside the scope of this book, but one might question whether entrepreneurial ministers are likely to undertake local, low-key, low-cost and potentially low-impact initiatives rather than larger projects because this leaves them in control of the situation rather than risking the death of an idea further up the hierarchy.

'To build something'

Bolton and Thompson include the phrase 'to build something' in their definition in order to describe the *aim* of the process referred to in the phrase 'habitually creates and innovates'. They explain that entrepreneurs 'build an entity that can be identified and is not just an idea or a concept though it may start that way'.[51] Entrepreneurial ministers are those who *do* things, or get things done, rather than those who have a hundred great ideas before breakfast and realize none of them.

The following part of Bolton and Thompson's definition has a bearing here. The building of the 'something' must be taken through to completion; moreover the 'something' that is built must be 'of recognized value'. For this to be the case, the work cannot be left half-finished.

'Of recognized value'

Bolton and Thompson point out that the generally held view of entrepreneurs is that they create financial capital. Their use of the phrase 'of recognized value', however, indicates that they want to broaden the definition beyond financial capital and 'expand upon the use of the word "entrepreneur" so that it also includes those who create social capital and aesthetic capital'.[52]

---

[51] Bolton and Thompson, *Entrepreneurs*, 17.
[52] Bolton and Thompson, *Entrepreneurs*, 17.

In a Grove Booklet, Bolton adds to these forms of capital 'spiritual capital', which he defines as 'All the Father's riches made available to the disciples of his Son, Jesus Christ, through the work of the Holy Spirit in the life of the believer'.[53] While explaining that the same talents are used to create all kinds of capital, however, he reminds us that in his view, entrepreneurs do not focus on capital. He argues that the target of entrepreneurs 'is to build something of recognized value. In the process they both use capital and create it but essentially it is a by-product of their building enterprise'.[54]

Drawing on the work of Francis Fukuyama, Bolton argues that spiritual capital can enhance social capital. Making reference to the Great Awakening of the nineteenth century, Fukuyama discusses the connection between Christian faith and transformed social conditions. He writes, 'In the battles against alcoholism, gambling, slavery, delinquency and prostitution and in the building of a dense network of voluntary institutions . . . ministers and lay believers were the foot soldiers'.[55] This view of the link between spiritual and social capital is echoed by Simms, who argues that those who catch God's entrepreneurial vision 'can become agents for change in families and communities [and] help connect people of faith to their divine mission of meeting needs of people in society'.[56] We might therefore expect to identify entrepreneurial ministers through evidence of the generation of spiritual and social capital at a congregational level. Moreover, if the congregation catches the vision for wider community transformation, we might expect to see evidence of the generation of social capital in the wider community.

'Around perceived opportunities'

Direction and focus are provided, argue Bolton and Thompson, by the inclusion of 'perceived opportunities'. The entrepreneur may not have original ideas, 'but spotting the opportunity to exploit the idea

---

[53] Bill Bolton, *The Entrepreneur and the Church*, Grove Pastoral Series, P107 (Cambridge: Grove Books, 2006), 21.

[54] Bolton, *Entrepreneur and the Church*, 19.

[55] Francis Fukuyama, *The Great Disruption: Human Nature and the Reconstitution of Social Order* (London: Profile Books, 1999), 16–17, cited in Bolton, *Entrepreneur and the Church*, 21.

[56] Simms, *Faith Entrepreneurs*, 20.

is a characteristic of the entrepreneur. Entrepreneurs see something others miss or only see in retrospect.'[57] Similarly, Simms states that 'A faith entrepreneur sees what others are blind to and dreams of new realities.'[58] Kirzner's approach to entrepreneurship, meanwhile, was marked out by an emphasis on 'alertness'; for Kirzner the profit gained by the successful entrepreneur was not a reward for bearing uncertainty but for being alert to, and taking action on, previously unnoticed opportunities. And in discussing Kirzner's focus on alertness, Ricketts reports that 'The gains from trade have to be *noticed* before they can be achieved.'[59]

Christian ministers are charged with sharing in the oversight of the Church, and I would suggest that a crucial aspect of exercising oversight is alertness.[60] The minister shares in the oversight of the Church to the end that the people of God may 'grow into the fullness of Christ'.[61] Facilitating this growth requires the minister to be, among other things, consistently alert to opportunities to undertake the task in new and appropriate ways. We might expect entrepreneurial ministers to demonstrate this alertness in very particular ways, providing an example of both the sorts of opportunities that might be taken (while noting that these will vary according to the minister's particular situation) and the type of approach that might be required in doing this.

---

[57] Bolton and Thompson, *Entrepreneurs*, 17.

[58] Simms, *Faith Entrepreneurs*, 21.

[59] Ricketts, in Casson et al., *Oxford Handbook*, 48 (italics mine).

[60] For a consideration of the oversight ministry of priests and bishops, see Steven Croft, *Ministry in Three Dimensions: Ordination and Leadership in the Local Church* (London: Darton, Longman and Todd, 1999), Part Four: 'Episcope: Ministry in the Third Dimension', 139–92.

[61] From *Common Worship: Ordination Services* (London: Church House Publishing, 2007), 32.

3

An entrepreneurial God?

I have written this book in the belief that entrepreneurs are a gift of God to the Church, and that in a time of discontinuous cultural change they have the potential to help the rest of us to recognize opportunities offered by the Holy Spirit and to step faithfully towards God's purposes. In this chapter I shall argue that an entrepreneurial approach to ministry and mission is consistent with some of the characteristics exhibited by God. I shall also identify and discuss significant figures in the Bible and Christian history who have adopted an entrepreneurial approach to collaborating with God.

I hope that, as we consider the possibility that God exhibits entrepreneurial qualities, this will help readers who still feel uncomfortable with the notion of entrepreneurship in the context of Christian ministry to see that these are the kind of character traits that we might expect to find in people created in the image of God, and that these traits can potentially be used for the glory of God and the furtherance of his kingdom. As you reflect on characters in Scripture and Christian history who have acted entrepreneurially, I hope you will be able to recognize that entrepreneurs have always been in our midst, helping the people of God to remain focused, engaged and faithful to their identity in the world.

The problem of talking about God

The use of language in relation to God is problematic. And using the language of entrepreneurship in relation to the characteristics that we might argue God exhibits is clearly no exception, since, like all language and ideas, entrepreneurship is a human construct. Ludwig Wittgenstein argues in *Tractatus Logico-Philosophicus* (first published in 1921) that any statement about God is nonsensical, stating that 'what we cannot speak about we must pass over in silence'.[1] More recently Alister McGrath asks 'How can God ever be described or discussed using human language?', and in response writes that 'Wittgenstein made this point forcefully: if human words are incapable of describing the distinctive aroma of coffee, how can they cope with something as subtle as God?'[2]

However, McGrath draws on Aquinas to argue that because God created the world there is an 'analogy of being' between God and the world, making it legitimate to use things in the created order as analogies for God. And in considering Aquinas' doctrine of analogy, he draws on Ian T. Ramsey's work, *Christian Discourse: Some Logical Explorations* (1965). Ramsey proposes that the range of analogies in Scripture each provide particular, although limited, insights, and that these interact with one another so that they together provide a coherent understanding of God. This leads McGrath to conclude that 'God, who is infinite, may be revealed in and through human words and finite images.'[3]

Mark McIntosh also considers the problem of talking about God. He discusses the need to 'think about God in ways that allow God to determine the meaning of our speech'[4] and says that 'Human words about God may become vessels provided by God and carrying the theologian from the shoreline of human meanings out into the unreachable depths of divine meaning.'[5]

Theologians have long wrestled with the problems inherent in the use of language and concepts in relation to God, but they concluded relatively early in Christian history that this does not prevent us from thinking or saying anything coherent in relation to God. In the context of this book, what emerges from reflection on the problematic nature of language and concepts in relation to God is the question of whether, in arguing that an entrepreneurial approach to Christian ministry is consistent with characteristics exhibited by God, we can apply to God any meaningful definition of the entrepreneur.

---

[1] Ludwig Wittgenstein, *Tractatus Logico-Philosophicus* (London: Routledge Classics, 2001), 8.

[2] Alister E. McGrath, *Christian Theology: An Introduction* (Oxford: Blackwell, 2001), 253.

[3] McGrath, *Christian Theology*, 255.

[4] Mark A. McIntosh, *Divine Teaching: An Introduction to Christian Theology* (Oxford: Blackwell, 2008), 33.

[5] McIntosh, *Divine Teaching*, 33.

I suggest that for the purposes of this chapter, which seeks to consider why we might usefully consider the potential contribution of entrepreneurial ministers to God's mission in the world, the following three points may be useful:

1 Because God has revealed himself to human beings, we may find meaningful and coherent ways of thinking and talking about him and his characteristics.
2 We may contend that an entrepreneurial approach to ministry is consistent with a way of viewing some of the characteristics exhibited by God.
3 Utilizing human concepts such as entrepreneurship as a lens through which to view God helps to deepen our understanding of him.

Although ultimately beyond the grasp of all language and understanding, the trinitarian God of the Christian faith reveals himself[6] to us in proclamation, in Scripture and in the person of Jesus Christ, the Word of God, whose teachings and actions invite understanding and response.[7] As Karl Barth writes, 'the Word of God means irrevocably and originally that God speaks.'[8] Since Christians believe that God has 'spoken', revealing himself to us 'through scriptural images and analogies'[9] and in the person of Jesus, we may state that it is possible to speak meaningfully and coherently about him, his attributes and the characteristics he exhibits. As we use language to seek a deeper understanding of God, we might therefore view entrepreneurship as 'an inadequate concept that we humbly employ as a pointer towards the divine reality, one which infinitely exceeds the grasp of our language, and is thus a form of analogy'.[10]

---

[6] In relation to God's revelation to human beings, Barth writes that 'men can know the Word of God'. Karl Barth, *Church Dogmatics: The Doctrine of the Word of God*, Vol. 1 (1.1) (Edinburgh: T. & T. Clark, 1956), 214.

[7] Barth writes that 'we regard the Word of God not merely as proclamation and Scripture but as God's revelation in proclamation and Scripture, we must regard it in its identity with God Himself. God's revelation is Jesus Christ, God's Son.' Barth, *Church Dogmatics*, Vol. 1, 155.

[8] Barth, *Church Dogmatics*, Vol. 1, 151.

[9] McGrath, *Christian Theology*, 255.

[10] McIntosh, *Divine Teaching*, 32. In relation to this point I note the position of Karl Barth, who stated that 'I regard the *analogia entis* as the invention of the Antichrist'. Barth, *Church Dogmatics*, Vol. 1, x.

Does the concept of entrepreneurship deepen our understanding of God?

While attempting to construct a plausible case for God exhibiting entrepreneurial qualities, we might usefully adopt a complementary line of enquiry, which is to ask whether the concept of entrepreneurship helps to deepen our understanding of God. Entrepreneurship is a concept that we are able to understand. We can imagine people acting entrepreneurially and discuss the nature of the activity in space and time. On this subject McGrath says helpfully, 'God is not an object or a person in space and time; nevertheless, such persons and objects can help us deepen our appreciation of God's character and nature.'[11]

Clearly entrepreneurship is not a 'person' or an 'object', but it is a recognizable set of behaviours based on particular character traits; one that, when undertaken successfully, has tangible results. In this sense, entrepreneurship is a concept that may serve to deepen our appreciation of God's character and nature. We can say, 'in His revelation of Himself to us, God seems to be a bit like this', and by way of illustration we might then outline some of the characteristics associated with entrepreneurship. If we are able to say that, among other things, God exhibits entrepreneurial characteristics, then we can plausibly suggest that some people, including lay or ordained ministers, might act in a like manner. It also follows that some, who are perhaps not natural entrepreneurs, might strive to act more entrepreneurially; by doing so they take their place within a rich Christian tradition of seeking to emulate the characteristics of God that are encountered through prayerful meditation on Scripture, observation of the example of other Christians, and the action of the Holy Spirit in the heart.

Does God exhibit entrepreneurial characteristics?

Drawing on the definitions of the entrepreneur explored in the previous chapter, I shall next consider the possibility that God exhibits entrepreneurial characteristics in relation to aspects of both my own definition:

---

[11] McGrath, *Christian Theology*, 255.

> A visionary who, in partnership in with God and others, chal-
> lenges the status quo by energetically creating and innovating
> in order to shape something of kingdom value.

and the definition proposed by Bolton and Thompson:

> A person who habitually creates and innovates to build some-
> thing of recognized value around perceived opportunities.

'A visionary who, in partnership with . . . others'

A visionary is someone who thinks about the future with imagination and wisdom. Visionaries have original ideas about what the
future could be like; they are able to conceive of an alternative reality
in which things are better for more of us than they are now. Since
God is outside time, considering the possibility that he 'thinks about
the future', and is therefore a visionary, is problematic. However, God
has created time and space – a supreme act of wisdom, imagination
and originality – and God is present to us in this realm of time and
space. Through the activity of the Holy Spirit, moreover, God has
inspired the Scriptures with their grand, sequential metanarrative
of creation, fall, redemption and the eventual establishment of his
dominion over all things at the end of the age. God also inspires
prophets who, even in our own time, articulate an alternative reality
and recall us to God's purposes for the whole of his creation. In this
sense, then, we can see that God reveals himself to us (we who are
currently bounded by time and space) as displaying characteristics
that we might describe as visionary.

We can therefore say not only that this aspect of my definition of
the entrepreneur is consistent with what God has chosen to reveal
of himself, but also that those who strive to follow him are called
to be a visionary people, or at least a people familiar with the possibility of a new and different future in which God's ways become
our ways.

I have suggested that an entrepreneur is a visionary 'in partnership with others'. It is not particularly difficult to argue that God
exhibits this aspect of entrepreneurship. We see his desire to partner with those he has created in the creation narrative in Genesis,
throughout the Old Testament, in the Gospel accounts of Jesus'
highly collaborative approach to ministry and in the work of the
Holy Spirit in the lives of the apostles and the believers who formed

the early Church. In our own time God continually provides us with the opportunity of partnership, and effective entrepreneurs echo this aspect of his being.

Of course there are plenty of entrepreneurs who act alone, drawing on their own resources to achieve their goals and aims. However, striving to engage in kingdom work on our own is rarely what is called for and without wider ownership it will generally yield minimal fruit. We note that when Noah set out to build an ark, he did so with his family. When Jesus sent out the seventy-two he sent them in pairs. Those who work in partnership with others as they undertake entrepreneurial activity are similarly able to multiply their effect. The approach and the subsequent results are then embedded in the lives of others.

I must sound a note of caution here, stating in the strongest possible terms that those who are entrepreneurial should completely resist the temptation to employ a rhetoric of partnership when in truth they are simply engaged in persuading others to go along with a particular plan or project. Manipulating others in order to achieve our own ends, however worthy we judge those ends to be, is unethical, ultimately counterproductive and should be avoided at all costs. Partnering with others 'to shape something of kingdom value' means working alongside others in a way that honours their contribution. Those who engage in entrepreneurial ministry for the sake of the kingdom of God must lay down pride and personal agendas. As we reflect on Jesus' approach to partnership and his insistence that he came not to be served but to serve, we are given an example that the entrepreneurs in our midst should take great care to emulate.

'A person'

Bolton and Thompson say that '"person" emphasizes that a personality, rather than a system, is involved';[12] Barth, meanwhile, writes that 'God's Word means that God speaks and this implies its personal quality'.[13] The mainstream denominations uphold the doctrine, rooted in Scripture, that God's being is trinitarian: God is Father,

---

[12] Bill Bolton and John Thompson, *Entrepreneurs: Talent, Temperament, Technique*, 2nd edn (Oxford: Elsevier, 2004), 16.

[13] Barth, *Church Dogmatics*, Vol. 1, 136.

Son and Holy Spirit.[14] The Nicene Creed, the Apostles' Creed and the Athanasian Creed are used by churches around the globe as doctrinal formulas, and each sets out God's being as trinitarian. The trinitarian being of God is also set out in Article 1 of the Articles of Religion, *Of Faith in the Holy Trinity*: 'in unity of this Godhead there be three Persons, of one substance, power, and eternity; the Father, the Son, and the Holy Ghost'.[15] The doctrine of the Trinity, of three Persons coexisting in unity, allows us to say that this first aspect of Bolton and Thompson's definition is consistent with what we have come to understand of God's being.

'Who challenges the status quo'

For anyone familiar with the narrative of Scripture, a consideration of whether 'challenging the status quo' is consistent with characteristics exhibited by God is relatively straightforward. In the Bible we see God partnering with a wide range of individuals and groups to consistently challenge the established order both within Israel and beyond. The Old Testament prophets, from Moses through to Malachi, continually challenge the people's efforts to establish an order based on alternatives to the lordship of YHWH. In the Gospels Jesus confronts the pride, unfaithfulness and hypocrisy that have come to characterize the religious establishment of his day and, as a visionary, he articulates the alternative reality of the coming kingdom of God. Inspired by the Spirit of God, the task of challenging the established order is continued by the apostles and the members of the early Church. So we may say that challenging the status quo is consistent with the being of God – and that in the context of Christian ministry it is an aspect of entrepreneurship which, although rarely comfortable, we should not be surprised to witness, or even be personally affected by!

'Energetically creating'/'who habitually creates'

As we have seen, Bolton and Thompson tell us that '"Habitually" is an important characteristic of entrepreneurs. The true entrepreneur

---

[14] In the third century Origen taught that God is 'Three Hypostases in one Ousia' – that is, three divine *hypostases* or persons (Father, Son and Holy Spirit), who are distinct from one another yet being of one *ousia*, or substance.

[15] <www.Churchofengland.org/prayer-worship/worship/book-of-common-prayer/articles-of-religion.aspx> (18/01/13).

just cannot stop being an entrepreneur.'[16] I have used the word 'energetically' to grasp something close to this, although my choice was also shaped by a desire to communicate the fact that entrepreneurs often seem to act out of a surplus of personal energy and this has the potential to be contagious, positively affecting others who are involved. In reflecting on God's interaction with his creation and his engagement with those with whom he has dealings, David Ford catches something of the way in which Bolton and Thompson use the word 'habitually' and I use 'energetically': 'there is always more, and God can go on springing surprises in history'.[17]

God's consistent, even persistent and energetic creativity as he engages with people and nations in the Bible cannot meaningfully be described as 'habitual', since habits are learnt behaviours and as such are particular to creatures rather than the creator. And, even though Bolton and Thompson imply a positive emphasis for the word, when used in relation to human beings it is generally encumbered by unhelpful baggage; it has connotations of behavioural practices that one cannot really help. In this sense, 'habitually' cannot be seen as consistent with the being of God. However, if we take something of the essence of the word as Bolton and Thompson deploy it in their definition – that is, to assist us in understanding that the entrepreneur is not someone who happens to act in this way once or twice, or brings a single good idea to life and then settles down, but rather a person who goes on creating as he or she acts entrepreneurially – then in this sense we might concede that this aspect of Bolton and Thompson's definition is consistent with a characteristic exhibited by God.

This is also true of my use of 'energetically'. In some sense we understand that the triune God is the energy at the heart of all that is seen and unseen. It is this energy which brings life into existence and sustains it moment by moment, which is responsible for resurrection and for continual renewal and refreshing. In this sense, my inclusion of 'energetically' is consistent with the being of God.

My intention in using the word 'energetically' was also to capture something of the way in which entrepreneurs are often driven by

---

[16] Bolton and Thompson, *Entrepreneurs*, 16.
[17] David F. Ford, *Theology: A Very Short Introduction* (Oxford: Oxford University Press, 1999), 36.

deep personal resources to move towards achieving particular goals, doing so again and again. Here too we see that this is consistent with the being of God who, having created, goes on creating and engaging and, as the prophet Isaiah writes, 'doing a new thing' (Isaiah 43.19).

Bolton and Thompson tell us that the word '"creates" is used to emphasize the fact that entrepreneurs start from scratch and bring into being something that was not there before'.[18] It is not overly challenging to argue that this aspect of both their definition and my own is consistent with a key characteristic exhibited by God. That God *creates* (Genesis 1.1) is the first thing we discover when we begin to read Genesis. We might say that God 'started from scratch'; we can certainly say that he brought 'into being something that was not there before'. In Genesis 1.2–3 we see this demonstrated in the creation of light, when previously there had been only darkness. The Church receives, accepts and teaches the doctrine of God as creator. The belief that God created all that exists is stated explicitly in the Nicene, Apostles' and Athanasian Creeds and in *Of Faith in the Holy Trinity*, Article 1, which names God as 'the Maker, and Preserver of all things both visible and invisible'.[19]

God's creativity is not just seen at the initial act of creation but continues to be evident throughout the story of Scripture, both in his interactions with individuals[20] and the nation of Israel, and in the incarnation of Jesus, including his life, teaching and miracles. We may argue that God's creativity, marked by his consistency in acting in unprecedented and 'game-changing' ways, is most profoundly and disturbingly evident in the resurrection of Jesus from the dead; a foretaste of the age to come in God's new creation (Revelation 21). Since his being and his doing are inseparable, God *is* creativity; he created, he creates and he goes on creating. The creativity of God will go on surprising us since it will always be unprecedented.[21] We may say, therefore, that the inclusion of 'creates' in both my own

---

[18] Bolton and Thompson, *Entrepreneurs*, 16.
[19] <www.Churchofengland.org/prayer-worship/worship/book-of-common-prayer/articles-of-religion.aspx> (18/01/13).
[20] Four examples are Noah (Genesis 9), Abram (Genesis 12), Moses (Exodus 3) and the Apostle Paul (Acts 9).
[21] We see evidence for this in Moses' encounter with God at the burning bush. God reveals His name as 'I AM WHO I AM,' or 'I WILL BE WHAT I WILL BE' (Exodus 3.14).

and Bolton and Thompson's definition is consistent with the being of God.

Before moving on to the next section I should note that human beings are created in the image, or likeness, of God (Genesis 1.27). Since creativity is not merely consistent with God's being but is a fundamental aspect of it, it follows that those whom he has created 'in his image' will, to some degree, possess and manifest the creator's desire and ability to create; in fact this is part of the rationale underpinning this section of the book. That is, if we can say that aspects of a definition of entrepreneurship are consistent with God's being, then we might reasonably expect to see such characteristics displayed in human beings and especially, perhaps, in those who seek to serve God.

Among many other characteristics that we might mention, creativity is manifest in the life and ministry of Jesus, who said about himself, 'I am in the Father and the Father is in me' (John 14.11) and 'Anyone who has seen me has seen the Father' (John 14.9b). In addition, Jesus said about his ministry, 'My teaching is not my own. It comes from the one who sent me' (John 7.16) and, 'Whoever believes in me, . . . rivers of living water will flow from within them' (John 7.38). Those who are baptized into Christ are 'in Christ Jesus' (Romans 8.1) and his Spirit dwells in them,[22] and as such they may expect to manifest creativity, first by virtue of having been created and further, because of their participation in God the Father through Jesus the Son as a result of the continuing work of the Holy Spirit in their hearts and minds.[23] It is this activity of the Spirit that both compels and enables those who are in Christ to strive to learn from him and copy his example in word and deed.[24]

And so, at a fundamental level, and in the broadest sense, we may expect to see some degree of creativity manifested in the lives of those

---

[22] 'For all of you who were baptised into Christ have clothed yourselves with Christ' (Galatians 3.27); 'There is now no condemnation for those who are in Christ Jesus . . . And if the Spirit of him who raised Jesus from the dead is living in you, he who raised Christ from the dead will also give life to your mortal bodies because of his Spirit who lives in you' (Romans 8.1, 11).

[23] 'But the mind governed by the Spirit is life and peace' (Romans 8.6b).

[24] Jesus tells his disciples, 'A new command I give you: love one another. As I have loved you, so you must love one another. By this everyone will know that you are my disciples, if you love one another' (John 13.34–35).

who profess to follow Christ. Those who are in Christ will exhibit their creativity in countless different ways and with varying degrees of competence. They will not be more or less creative than those who do not profess to follow Christ, but Scripture leads us to understand that the God-given creativity of those who are in Christ is being daily shaped by the activity of the Holy Spirit and increasingly brought under the Lordship of Christ and used in the service of the kingdom. This God-given creativity, therefore, is being sanctified, and this ongoing sanctification is a collaborative process in which those who are in Christ strive continually to cooperate with the work of the Spirit within them.

But the exercise of entrepreneurship involves more than creativity. Entrepreneurs make use of their God-given creativity alongside a range of other gifts and competencies. I have suggested that, since God created human beings in his image, we might expect to see evidence of creativity, however small, in each human life and that this creativity is being sanctified in the lives of those who are in Christ. Creativity is one aspect of both my own and Bolton and Thompson's definitions and we may certainly say that it is a characteristic both of God and of human beings. However, if all human beings have the potential to exercise creativity, it does not follow that all have the potential to act entrepreneurially.

'And innovates . . .'

As a phenomenon, innovation has been around for as long as people have walked the earth. It is part of our created nature to think of new ways of doing things and to try them out. Early innovations include clothing, agriculture and alphabets, while more recent ones include printing, the internal combustion engine, telecommunications and the internet. Without innovation our world would be a very different place.

We should be aware, though, that innovating is not the same as inventing. Invention is the creative process involved in having a new idea for a product or process, while innovation is the attempt to bring that new idea into existence. Joseph Schumpeter defined innovation as new combinations of existing resources; and he believed that it was entrepreneurs who were able to undertake this activity.

This is a fundamental component of the definition of the entrepreneur, but it is an aspect that proves problematic when applied to God. Since God's *being* and his *doing* cannot be separated,[25] what is brought into existence by God is, because of the nature of its creator, perfect. In my view therefore, the concept of innovation cannot meaningfully be applied to God. Having created, God cannot innovate in order to improve on what he has created.

However, God is distinct from what he has created, so that human beings have the capacity to utilize imagination to think creatively – about a problem, for example – and innovate in order to find a solution. The ability to engage in innovation allows human beings to collaborate creatively with God in a created order that is subject to decay and in which God's kingdom is coming but has not yet been fully realized. The need for innovation is a reminder that it is the nature of things in their current state to be in flux rather than equilibrium.[26] The desire and ability to innovate should serve to remind human beings that they are creatures rather than the creator.

'To shape something of kingdom value'/'build something of recognized value'

I chose to use the word 'shape' in my definition because I was keen to steer clear of any reference to entrepreneurs engaging in empire building. It is also the case that in the context of the Church and its ministry, 'shaping' evokes the sense that what is being undertaken is a collaborative effort, one in which entrepreneurs make a contribution to shaping what God and others are also involved in bringing into being.

Next, when entrepreneurs engage in entrepreneurial activity they do so with an aim. 'Something' needs to result from their efforts and it should be of some value to others. In the context of Christian ministry I felt that this was best expressed as 'kingdom value', meaning that in some way the efforts of the entrepreneur contribute to the furtherance of God's coming kingdom of justice, provision, wholeness, peace and reconciliation.

Similarly, when they talk about 'recognized value' Bolton and Thompson aim to 'broaden the definition from the purely commercial'.[27] They provide the example of Dr Barnardo, who created social

---

[25] Again we may note God's revelation of his name to Moses: 'I AM WHO I AM' or, 'I WILL BE WHAT I WILL BE' (Exodus 3.14).

[26] 'For this world in its present form is passing away' (1 Corinthians 7.31b).

[27] Bolton and Thompson, *Entrepreneurs*, 17.

capital, explaining that 'While his [Dr Barnardo's] motive may have been philanthropy, he was only able to achieve what he did because he was an entrepreneur.'[28]

In the beginning God created the heavens and the earth and gave human beings a mandate to multiply and spread out over the earth and to steward his creation: essentially to build something of *kingdom* or *recognized* value. We might say that, among other things, the writer of Genesis 1 sets out to teach the reader that human beings, created in the image of God, are to use the resources with which he has blessed them, including their creativity, in the fulfilment of a task that will require them to act energetically, habitually, creatively and innovatively with respect to countless perceived opportunities over the course of human history. The narrative of Scripture points to God's intention that those whom he has created should collaborate with him, over time and across nations, in building things of recognized, kingdom and therefore eternal value. In this sense, we may say that my own and Bolton and Thompson's definitions are consistent in this aspect with characteristics exhibited by God: God creates and recognizes the value of what he has spoken into being,[29] and human beings, also (generally) recognizing the value of the created order and their own existence within it,[30] strive to build things of recognized value, sometimes collaborating with God[31] (*kingdom value*) and at other times in spite of him.[32]

It is interesting to note that when considering the possibility of 'recognized value' in relation to God, the narrative of Scripture provides a picture of God's covenant people, Israel, persistently failing or refusing to recognize the existence, presence or authority of God and instead worshipping the gods of other nations.[33] Directly related to this is the fact that although all of what Jesus did was of kingdom

---

[28] Bolton and Thompson, *Entrepreneurs*, 17.

[29] 'God saw all that he had made, and it was very good' (Genesis 1.31).

[30] As David demonstrates in the words of Psalm 8.

[31] 'Always give yourselves fully to the work of the Lord, because you know that your labour in the Lord is not in vain' (1 Corinthians 15.58).

[32] As we see set out in the description of 'the wicked man' in Psalm 10.2–11.

[33] Numerous Scripture references could be provided in support of this point. As an example I cite the following, taken from the second chapter of Judges, and setting out what followed the death of Joshua: 'After [Joshua's death], another generation grew up who knew neither the LORD nor what he had done for Israel. Then the Israelites did evil in the eyes of the LORD and served the Baals. They forsook the LORD, the God of their ancestors' (Judges 2.10–12).

value, much of his ministry went widely unrecognized, particularly by those in religious authority in Israel. The details of his humble birth, far from centres of power and people of influence; his childhood in a poverty-stricken village in an insignificant corner of the Roman Empire; his execution as a young man after a brief and localized public ministry alongside petty criminals, with the accompanying implication that he achieved nothing except his own annihilation – all, we might say, are the opposite of recognition!

The writer of John's Gospel highlights this, stating that 'though the world was made through him, the world did not recognise him. He came to that which was his own, but his own did not receive him' (John 1.10). Within Scripture this rejection is set in the context of the overarching purposes of God and ultimately, the establishment of his kingdom and the bringing of all things under the Lordship of Jesus Christ.[34] In this sense, Jesus' own (entrepreneurial) approach to life and ministry was of absolute kingdom value. In considering whether the 'recognized value' in Bolton and Thompson's definition is consistent with the being of God, we might observe that the activity of God among those whom he has created has been frequently dismissed and has failed to have 'recognized value'. This is in spite of the fact that there are many who do recognize the value of the work of God, and ultimately all *will* recognize, if not the value, then at least God's claim of ultimate authority over all things.

Entrepreneurs in the Bible

We can identify various figures in the Bible and in Christian history whose faith in God has resulted in their adopting what might be described as an entrepreneurial approach to their collaboration with God.

'See, I have placed before you an open door that no one can shut' (Revelation 3.8). Bill Bolton draws on this verse from Revelation to suggest that the church in Philadelphia, to whom the words are addressed, 'served a God of the open door as do we'.[35] Bolton tells us that 'It should not therefore surprise us to find a strong

---

[34] Revelation 21 provides a powerful image of God's ultimate intention for the created order.

[35] Bill Bolton, *The Entrepreneur and the Church*, Grove Pastoral Series, P107 (Cambridge: Grove Books, 2006), 5.

entrepreneurial theme running through the Bible. Entrepreneurship is nothing new to the Church; we have a substantial heritage.'[36]

Bolton names a number of figures in the Bible whom he argues were entrepreneurs, including Noah, Abram, Jacob, Joshua, Caleb, David, Jesus and Paul. He argues that these characters display entrepreneurial qualities: that they take risks, face challenges, spot opportunities, find innovative solutions to problems, challenge the status quo, make a difference and build something of recognized value. And he goes on to say that entrepreneurship is in the DNA of the Church; he writes that, after the resurrection of Jesus, 'the coming of the Holy Spirit at Pentecost is a remarkable entrepreneurial story. The book of Acts is a description of entrepreneurs in action.'[37]

I would add other examples to Bolton's list, including Nimrod (Genesis 10.8–12), Joseph, Moses, Rahab (Joshua 2), Ehud (Judges 3.12–30), Gideon (Judges 6—8), Ruth, Abigail (1 Samuel 25), Elijah, Elisha, Jehoshaphat (1 Kings 22.41–48; 2 Chronicles 17—20), Hezekiah (2 Kings 18; 2 Chronicles 29—32), Josiah (2 Kings 22—23; 2 Chronicles 34—35), Ezra, Nehemiah, and the Wife of Noble Character (Proverbs 31.10–31). There are many others, however, who feature in the narrative of Scripture but are not accompanied by evidence of what could realistically be described as an entrepreneurial approach to their efforts at collaborating with God. Examples might include Noah's sons, Isaac, the sons of Jacob (excluding Joseph), various judges, kings, priests, prophets and countless 'ordinary' people. The Bible is the prominent source of authority for Christians.[38] By providing examples, therefore, of individuals in Scripture whom we might argue demonstrate entrepreneurial characteristics we can suggest that this is a faithful approach to collaborating with God and one that has a long heritage. As discussed above, recognizing the presence of entrepreneurial individuals in the Bible is helpful both because it has the potential to deepen our

---

[36] Bolton, *Entrepreneur and the Church*, 5.

[37] Bolton, *Entrepreneur and the Church*, 6.

[38] Article 6 of the Articles of Religion states that 'Scripture contains all things necessary to salvation'. <www.Churchofengland.org/prayer-worship/worship/book-of-common-prayer/articles-of-religion.aspx#VI> (23/01/13). Alan Bartlett writes, 'Scripture is reaffirmed in the Lambeth Quadrilateral, as the first of Anglicanism's non-negotiables, and in the Declaration of Assent as the place of unique revelation. It is the ultimate point of reference.' Alan Bartlett, *A Passionate Balance: The Anglican Tradition* (London: Darton, Longman and Todd, 2007), 91.

understanding of the being of God, and because it lends validity to the idea that an entrepreneurial approach to ministry warrants serious and prayerful reflection on the part of those who seek to serve God faithfully in every age. Since the Bible contains examples of people acting entrepreneurially, we might expect to see examples of Christian ministers acting entrepreneurially in our own time too.

With the exception of Jesus, there are aspects of the lives of each of those listed above that may deserve added consideration before we attempt to emulate them. However, the intention here is to provoke reflection on the way in which these individuals adopted an entrepreneurial approach to their collaboration with God rather than on the less savoury, or culturally awkward, aspects of their behaviour.

Entrepreneurs in Christian history

In addition to the examples found in the Bible, as a response to their faith in God thousands of individuals throughout the course of Christian history have adopted an entrepreneurial approach to collaborating with him. From what we know of their lives and from reflecting on the effect and legacy of their actions, some helpful examples, from early Christian history to the present day, are set out below.

These entrepreneurial Christians have been chosen on the basis that they are relatively well known. The list is neither objective nor exclusive, and an equally effective list of examples could have been comprised of entirely different names. But as we reflect on what we know of their lives, and consider their approach to collaborating with God and the fact that as a result of spotting opportunities, using their creativity, engaging in innovation and taking risks they all built during their lifetimes things of recognized value whose effects continue to have a positive impact on the lives of others, I contend that we might refer to these people as entrepreneurs.

As with those who have been given as examples of entrepreneurs in the Bible, there are aspects of the lives of some of these people that might appear awkward or culturally challenging in the light of contemporary values and approaches to working with others. A number of them were criticized by their contemporaries for their domineering presence, their headstrong approach, their ignoring of protocol or their failure to observe correct procedures. However, as with the

An entrepreneurial God?

examples taken from the Bible, the purpose of drawing attention to these people is to support the claim that the exercise of entrepreneurial approach to ministry in the present is consistent with Christian activity across the centuries. Acting entrepreneurially in the service of God has a significant heritage and it is an approach that we might expect to see wherever the people of God are active in the service of the kingdom.

The list is as follows:

St Patrick, bishop, missionary and evangelist in Ireland in the second half of the fifth century.

St Francis of Assisi (1181–1226), who founded the Franciscan Order, the Second Order of St Francis (the Order of St Clare) and the Third Order of St Francis.

St Clare of Assisi (1194–1253), founder of the Order of Poor Ladies (renamed the Order of St Clare after her death) and the first woman to author a monastic rule.

St Teresa of Ávila (1515–82), Spanish Carmelite nun, reformer of the Carmelite Order and co-founder with John of the Cross of the Discalced Carmelites, as well as a mystic, theologian and writer in the Counter-Reformation.

Count Nikolaus Ludwig von Zinzendorf (1700–60), religious and social reformer in Germany and bishop in the Moravian Church.

John Wesley (1703–91), Anglican cleric, theologian and co-founder of the Methodist movement.

William Carey (1761–1834), Baptist minister and missionary to India, also the co-founder of the Baptist Missionary Society and a Bible translator.

Elizabeth Fry (1780–1845), Quaker, philanthropist and visionary prison and social reformer.

William Booth (1829–1912) and **Catherine Booth** (1829–90), co-founders of the Salvation Army and pioneers of social and spiritual reform.

Dr John Barnardo (1845–1905), philanthropist and the founder and director of Barnardo's children's homes.

Toyohiko Kagawa (1888–1960), Japanese pacifist, labour activist, reformer and founder of many churches, hospitals and schools.

Rick Warren, contemporary American pastor and author, also the founder of Saddleback megachurch in California.

Les Isaac, London-based founder of the Street Pastors initiative, set up in 2003 and currently present in 280 towns and cities across eight countries.

Ann Marie Wilson, founder of '28 Too Many', a UK-based charity striving to eradicate female genital mutilation (FGM) in 28 African countries.

Neil Cole, American church leader and author, the founder and director of Church Multiplication Associates and CMA Resources.

Mike Breen, English church leader and author, also the founder of 3DM Ministries, a cross-denominational learning network of churches.

Jessie Joe Jacobs, founder and first chief executive of 'A Way Out', an outreach and prevention charity based in Stockton-on-Tees and specializing in engaging vulnerable and hard to reach women and young people.

Rich Jones, chief executive of the Joshua Project, a youth initiative based in Bradford working with underprivileged children and young people.

Not all are entrepreneurs

I am not suggesting that because entrepreneurship may be consistent with some of the characteristics displayed by God we should expect all ministers, all Christians or all human beings to be entrepreneurs or to act entrepreneurially. The evidence seems to contradict such a position. Bolton cites studies that show just 10 to 15 per cent of people in the UK are entrepreneurs, although he argues that more entrepreneurs might emerge if the conditions were right. Indeed, Michael Moynagh argues that the likely figure is in fact far higher; even if Moynagh's sense is correct, however, and the number of entrepreneurs in our churches is higher than Bolton suggests, we may still say that entrepreneurs do not make up the majority of the population.

I have given some examples of entrepreneurial individuals in the Bible and Christian history. Yet even if it were possible to refer to the hundreds of thousands of individuals who, throughout history, have expressed their faith in God by acting entrepreneurially, there have been millions of others who served God in other ways. Entrepreneurs achieve wildly different things, but they share an approach to life and a way of behaving that is common only to a relatively small proportion of us. Entrepreneurs in Scripture and Christian history are catalysts for change and growth. Bolton refers to them as 'the leaven that affects the whole'.[39] I believe that they are, in essence, a gift of God to the majority;[40] as the individuals I have listed demonstrate, their actions have the potential to be of lasting benefit both to the people of God[41] and to the wider community.

---

[39] Bolton, *Entrepreneur and the Church*, 4.

[40] Bolton does however argue that entrepreneurs are not always able to act as 'leaven': 'The leaven is not able to do its job because our institutions and bureaucratic systems prevent it. They have declared the entrepreneur redundant.' Bolton, *Entrepreneur and the Church*, 4.

[41] Paul points out in 1 Corinthians 12.27–30 that his readers are the body of Christ, that each has a part and that a variety of gifts are distributed to the members of the body by God for the service and benefit of the whole.

Part 2

DREAMING DREAMS, BUILDING REALITY: ENTREPRENEURIAL MINISTERS IN THEIR OWN WORDS

4

Facets of the entrepreneur

In Part 1 of this book I addressed the reservations that some Christians have with the concept of entrepreneurship in relation to Christian ministry. I considered a positive understanding of the entrepreneur, showing that lay and ordained entrepreneurial ministers are a gift of God whose contribution to both the Church and wider community will be particularly valuable at a time of rapid and discontinuous cultural change. I explored how God demonstrates characteristics associated with entrepreneurship and that an entrepreneurial approach to ministry and mission is one that we are not only able to see in the Bible and Christian history but should expect to see in our own times too.

In Part 2, I shall first briefly explain the approach I took to researching entrepreneurial ministers (my methodology), and then discuss six important themes that emerged from my research. Part 2 also includes suggestions about what the Church can do to encourage and provide resources for an entrepreneurial approach to ministry and mission and an outline of potentially fruitful avenues for further research.

Who participated in my research?

As I mentioned in the Introduction, all research has limitations and mine was no exception. Time and access were significant considerations, as I was conducting my research alongside a demanding full-time teaching post and had three young children at home! I therefore made the decision to focus on ordained Anglican priests ministering in parishes in the Diocese of Durham. I did not engage with entrepreneurial lay ministers, although I have already noted the importance of encouraging entrepreneurship in such ministers and I hope that some readers will be able to engage in research in this area. Although the focus of my research was on ordained entrepreneurial ministers, however, the findings will be useful to any Christian seeking to understand what entrepreneurship might contribute to faithful and effective ministry and mission today.

I first approached the Bishop of Jarrow and asked if he would support and participate in the study. Once we had met and discussed entrepreneurship in depth, the bishop provided me with the names of 16 parish priests in the Diocese of Durham who, in his view, were adopting an entrepreneurial approach to their ministries.[1] These were men and women of a variety of ages and spiritualities and with varying lengths of service and seniority. All agreed to take part in the research, which involved taking an online test (discussed below) designed to identify potential entrepreneurs and participating in two in-depth interviews. The Bishop of Jarrow himself agreed to participate, as did the then Bishop of Durham, Justin Welby, which made a total sample of 18 participants.

Working with these 18 was encouraging and inspiring. It also generated a vast amount of data. In order to have a reasonable chance of producing worthwhile findings within the available time frame I had to find a way to reduce the data to a more manageable scale, so I decided to focus on the data generated by the seven respondents who achieved 'outstanding' scores in their online test. The themes discussed in the following chapters emerged from the data generated by these seven, highly entrepreneurial parish priests.

Clearly I had to ask myself whether findings generated from work with seven individuals would be valid. Since the research did not aim to generate findings from which I intended to generalize, however, but instead to produce suggestions whose usefulness in their own situation readers might be able to judge, I felt that the 18 ministers with whom I initially worked, and then the seven who formed the eventual focus, comprised a sample small enough to work with in the time available yet large enough to generate a useful volume and depth of data. As readers, you will have to judge to what extent my findings and the suggestions that emerge from them are transferable to the context in which you may be seeking to minister.

---

[1] I discuss the strengths and limitations of this approach to generating a research sample in my doctoral thesis ('An Entrepreneurial Approach to Priestly Ministry in the Parish: Insights from a Research Study in the Diocese of Durham' (unpublished PhD thesis, Durham University, 2013)). It should be added that the bishop did not name the only entrepreneurial ministers in the diocese but the 16 who came to mind on that occasion.

How did I arrive at my findings?

Worthwhile research findings emerge from good analysis of data. My data came from two sources: an online tool and interviews. The online tool, designed by Bolton and Thompson, identifies six entrepreneurial character themes, which can be summed up in the acronym FACETS. Bolton and Thompson claim that the themes can be measured and therefore form a basis for identifying potential entrepreneurs. The six themes are as follows:[2]

1 *Focus.* The ability to lock on to a target and not be distracted, to act with urgency and not procrastinate, to get things done and not just talk about them.
2 *Advantage.* The ability to select the right opportunity and to pick winners.
3 *Creativity.* The ability to come up with new ideas habitually. This allows entrepreneurs to think differently and to see patterns others miss.
4 (a) *Ego (inner).* Provides confidence, creates passion and delivers the motivation to achieve and win.
  (b) *Ego (outer).* The ability to carry heavy responsibility lightly but not flippantly, to be openly accountable and instinctively courageous.
5 *Team.* The ability to pick the best people and get them working as a team, to know when you need help and to find it, to build an extensive network of supporters. This facet provides the entrepreneur's multiplier effect.
6 *Social.* The ability to espouse a cause and deliver on it. This is the distinguishing facet of the social entrepreneur.[3]

Bolton and Thompson point out that the first four facets (which form the acronym FACE) are essential for entrepreneurs and that it is not possible to be a successful entrepreneur without them.

The last two, however, *team* and *social*, are not found in all entrepreneurs. Bolton and Thompson argue that some entrepreneurs create followers but not teams, but those who are strong on *team* are able to multiply the effect of their entrepreneurial efforts by building

---

[2] Bill Bolton and John Thompson, *Entrepreneurs: Talent, Temperament, Technique*, 2nd edn (Oxford: Elsevier, 2004), 51.
[3] Summary of FACETS from Bolton and Thompson, *Entrepreneurs*, 51–2.

and facilitating a strong team. The *social* facet is unique to the social entrepreneur and is, along with *ego*, a matter of temperament. Bolton and Thompson suggest that temperamental facets are the most crucial and argue that 'There is just no point in starting along the entrepreneur road without a strong *ego* facet to keep you going and make the journey a fulfilling and successful experience.'[4]

By contrast, *focus*, *advantage*, *creativity* and *team* are talents; Bolton and Thompson suggest that 'we have them whether we like it or not but they must be discovered, nurtured and developed if they are to achieve their full potential.'[5]

The six character themes constitute the facets of the entrepreneur. According to Bolton and Thompson it is possible to measure a person against these facets and assess his or her entrepreneurial potential. The *First Screening Entrepreneur Indicator* (FSEI) is a set of balanced questions that participants answer online, receiving instant feedback that includes a score out of 10 for each character theme. Bolton and Thompson describe the FSEI as necessarily short and approximate. The strengths of respondents' facet character themes are derived from their responses to the questions. The results of the FSEI do not specify that the participant definitely has the potential to be an entrepreneur but rather that he or she *may* have the potential.

Those being considered for selection as Ordained Pioneer Ministers in the Church of England take the FSEI. This is because the OPM selection criteria state the need for potential OPMs to demonstrate entrepreneurial potential. The FSEI has also been used with 'regular' clergy in the Anglican dioceses of Chelmsford and Southwell as part of their leadership development programmes.[6] These factors are important because they make it possible to state that the tool has a relevant (albeit relatively limited) track record in a church context.

I invited each of my participants to take the FSEI. The scores they achieved for each character theme informed our subsequent interviews, providing a basis for discussion and reflection and a platform for exploration of each respondent's experience as an entrepreneur. I began analysing my data as soon as I began to generate it. Once each participant had completed the FSEI and taken part in

---

[4] Bolton and Thompson, *Entrepreneurs*, 52.
[5] Bolton and Thompson, *Entrepreneurs*, 52.
[6] Information provided by Bill Bolton via email, 23/01/12.

an in-depth interview, I made observations and notes and, as I read and re-read the transcripts, I began to make comparisons and to highlight emerging patterns. I engaged in thematic analysis of the data[7] which involved looking for commonalities, differences and relationships.

From analysis of the data I identified a number of themes, six of which are discussed in the following chapters, and from these emerged a number of suggestions for encouraging the exercise of entrepreneurship in the wider Church. The six key themes are as follows:

1 Respondents were highly positive about the use of the term 'entrepreneur' in relation to Christian ministry.
2 Respondents perceived church buildings as a potential resource.
3 Respondents naturally partnered and worked with others.
4 Respondents articulated a number of factors that they felt might aid the exercise of entrepreneurship in local churches and communities.
5 Respondents articulated a number of factors that they felt might hinder the exercise of entrepreneurship in local churches and communities.
6 Respondents articulated opinions about the extent to which the presence (or lack) of entrepreneurship in the senior leadership at regional and national level might affect the exercise of entrepreneurship in local churches and communities.

The respondents

In the following six chapters I discuss in some depth the interview responses of seven ordained entrepreneurial ministers. All seven were university graduates; each participant has been given a pseudonym and I have listed these below with some basic relevant information. The details are as close as possible to the respondents' actual circumstances but have been carefully amended to make positive identification of individuals as unlikely as possible.

Dan, 46. Vicar of a large suburban parish. Entered ordained ministry aged 25 after an early career in finance.

---

[7] Jamie Harding, *Qualitative Data Analysis From Start to Finish* (London: Sage, 2013), 4.

Jane, 50. Rector of a large urban parish. Entered ordained ministry aged 28 after spending a number of years living with a religious order.

Jim, 42. Recently licensed as vicar of two rural parishes. Entered ordained ministry aged 39 after a successful career in retail.

Matt, 54. Recently licensed as vicar of two suburban parishes. Entered ordained ministry aged 48 after a successful career as a corporate executive.

Roger, 60. Vicar of a large urban parish. Entered ordained ministry after graduating from university, aged 24.

Rupert, 53. Vicar of three suburban and two rural parishes. Area dean. Entered ordained ministry aged 40 after a successful career in an innovative international company.

Susan, 42. Vicar of a large suburban parish. Entered ordained ministry aged 36 after a successful career in education.

5

Feeling positive about entrepreneurs in Christian ministry

I asked each of my interviewees how they felt about the use of the term 'entrepreneur' in relation to Christian ministry. Without exception, all of them were positive. Roger felt that to bring the word into the vocabulary of the Church would 'do us a lot of good'. Matt explained that what was being described fitted him 'to a tee'. And Rupert said that the word 'describes in a very real way something which I understand from within'.

Although positive about entrepreneurship in relation to Christian ministry, however, Matt, Jane, Rupert and Jim each referred to the fact that others might not share this positive perception of the concept. Jane said simply, 'I have no problem with it but I can see why others do.' In spite of being positive, Jim's response betrayed something of his own reservation: 'My head tells me this is absolutely right. My heart tells me, hang on, pause and stop and think about this.' Jim explained that his hesitation was a result of the association of the term with making money (an issue addressed at some length in Chapter 1).

Rupert pointed out that there was no other word that served the same function, and said that it was a useful word in some conversations and would be a relevant thing for the wider Church to explore. He went on to say:

> People who don't inhabit the place of the entrepreneur think of it as people who turn a fast buck; somehow unscrupulous, not necessarily very principled. They start businesses and go bust and employees suffer and they end up with the big house and big car. I can't think of any other label off the top of my head that would work nearly as well. It's a 'use with caution among the right audiences' kind of word, really.

Matt outlined the way in which he viewed himself as an entrepreneur but learnt, as he entered the discernment process for ordained ministry in the Church of England, to underemphasize that aspect of himself:

> I learnt pretty early on in that process that you didn't use that word, that it was a word that made people wary of you. It was like a danger word. And so you found other ways of describing it. You wouldn't call yourself an entrepreneur because the Church would feel uncomfortable. That's how I was made to feel, that the Church would feel uncomfortable, bringing through into ordained ministry people who fundamentally saw themselves as entrepreneurs. It seemed like a quality that belonged to a different world, not the world of ordained ministry.

It is interesting that, against a background of the kind of perceived institutional negativity towards entrepreneurial ministers articulated by Matt, Susan expressed the opinion that all ordained ministers should be entrepreneurs. She said that 'all ordained people should be pioneering and responding to their communities', and added, 'If there's not something of this in each of us we have no business leading community.'

In his response Matt too went on to argue that acting entrepreneurially was essential for ordained ministers. He qualified this by saying,

> What the Church doesn't need is thick-skinned, task-orientated, low-accountability, headstrong leaders. I've seen those operating and that's part of my reserve, if you like, about ever wanting to dub myself an entrepreneur. I don't want to be saying I'm one of those headstrong, determined people who manipulate others and drive things along. I don't do that at all.

However, he followed this by reflecting on the situation in which he was engaged in ministry as an ordained minister:

> But when you reinterpret that in a context like the place I minister in, you think it's absolutely what the Church needs. Here and in loads and loads of places. People who can focus on what they're trying to achieve, who can spot what will work and what won't work, who can see new possibilities where people only see dead ends. We need that left, right and centre if the Church is going to get itself up off its complete uppers. Because without it, just care and maintenance without any adequate entrepreneurial drive, I fear for the Church, actually.

Matt's response to this question provoked reflection on the calling of the Church in the UK and on the nature, scope and urgency of the missional task it currently faces. More specifically, it provoked reflection on the various ways in which the denominations understand ordained ministry, the categories by which they select candidates for ordination or authorized leadership and the implicit messages candidates receive as they are processed through the system. The fact that when asked to respond to the use of the word 'entrepreneur' in relation to ordained Anglican ministry, Matt chose to expand on feeling that he needed to conceal this aspect of his nature is significant. His intuitive sense that revealing his entrepreneurial nature would make those involved in his selection uncomfortable must provoke us to ask whether, in fact, the Church of England and other mainstream denominations do have some prejudice towards entrepreneurial candidates for ordination – and, if they do, whether this prejudice is communicated explicitly or whether it is implied in the general approach to discernment, the literature candidates are encouraged to read, the nature of the questions they are asked, the areas on which they are asked to reflect and the criteria against which they are considered.

In his responses Matt explained that the situation in which he found himself as a minister could justifiably be described as desperate. One of his buildings required expensive repairs, he had dwindling and elderly congregations and a local community blighted by wide-ranging social problems. Matt rightly pointed out that if the Church in that particular place was to realize a hopeful future, it required entrepreneurial leadership. Based on my engagement both with current mission literature and local and national mission forums, networks and conferences, I would suggest that, with the exception of London, Matt's situation is replicated in communities across the United Kingdom.

Entrepreneurial ministers are not a 'quick-fix' solution for the various challenges that the mainstream denominations are currently struggling with. We do not require heroic individuals to save the day. However, those candidates offering themselves for ministry and who have entrepreneurial ability should be encouraged to demonstrate and to explore this aspect of their nature. Church leaders both nationally and locally, along with those involved in discerning vocation and overseeing selection processes, would do well to consider how they might communicate a positive response to those with entrepreneurial flair who present themselves for consideration for ministry.

And while churches must continue to recognize the need to select, train and ordain individuals for pioneering ministries, we must also avoid the temptation of assuming that the only ministers with entrepreneurial flair are pioneers. Pioneers are required to demonstrate entrepreneurial ability, but if churches limit the acceptance and encouragement of entrepreneurship to pioneers we risk missing out on a significant release of energy in other aspects of local ministry. Within the Church of England this means understanding the importance of selecting, training and deploying entrepreneurial parish priests, or at the very least clergy and key lay people who understand the importance of an entrepreneurial approach to ministry and mission and are able to identify and release those members of congregations who are able to act entrepreneurially. It is parish ministry that remains, after all, the central focus of much of the Church of England's strategy and the locus of its efforts in terms of ministry and mission.

6

Church buildings can be a resource

During their interviews over two-thirds of my respondents discussed issues relating to the buildings occupied by the churches of which they were a part. I found this particularly interesting since in the interviews I didn't ask directly about church buildings.

Roger and Dan had served in their parishes for over a decade and during that time both had to close one of the two church buildings that they started out with. In her previous post Jane had been involved in a multi-million pound building project which involved the church being demolished and rebuilt along with a community centre, doctor's surgery, offices for social services, housing, an elderly people's day care centre, a children's centre and a computer centre. At the time of our interviews Matt was facing the prospect of closing one of the two churches for which he was responsible. Jim, relatively new in post, was dealing with a broken heating system in his church as well as sharing the building with another local congregation whose own building had become unsafe.

Yet none of the ministers who talked about issues with their church buildings complained or spoke negatively about this. Roger and Dan both viewed the closure of buildings as opportunities and had seen positive involvement with local schools as a result. Jane spoke at length about the process of rebuilding and the ways in which this led to growth in her own skills, positive engagement with the local authority and community, better provision for the local community and a more appropriate and effective church building. Matt, whose building required repairs the cost of which was estimated at £100,000, was considering ways in which this could become a source of engagement with the local community. Jim viewed his issues with heating and the sharing of his building as opportunities to deepen relationships and work collaboratively.

In the responses of the ministers who spoke about issues with their church buildings it was possible to identify various entrepreneurial traits. In Roger's comments about closing a church building and re-evaluating engagement with the local primary school, we see a person perceiving an opportunity and building something of kingdom value by adopting a creative and innovative approach. In the FSEI Roger scored 7.7 for Creativity, 8.4 for Advantage and 10 for Team. These strengths were in evidence in his own narrative, particularly the high Team score, since by using 'we' throughout his response, Roger implies that this was a collaborative effort:

> We were closing a parish church that happened to be geographically close to, and very much involved with, one of the local primary schools, and we were going from two church buildings to one. This easy connection between the school and the place of worship was being lost but at the same time we were thinking we needed a new beginning for schools-based work. At about that time the Godly Play resource fell into the basket of possibilities and it works, and we've had lots of really profound time exploring the Bible with children for a few years. So we kept the connection with the school, and going to one church building and one congregation in fact released a whole lot of energy for ministry in the school and out there, as compared with previous Christian service keeping the show on the road and being burdened with buildings.

Dan spoke of being helped through the more challenging aspects of closing a church building by members of his church. Dan also scored a maximum 10 in the Team facet of the FSEI, and in the following comment we see evidence of someone who has built a strong team with whom to exercise ministry:

> If I'd not had a team of trusted colleagues that I love dearly I wouldn't have managed it as well as I did. They took ownership of it and they protected me from some of the things that happened. And the pastoral element of it has been marvellous.

Jane scored a maximum 10 on Focus. When I asked her about this she immediately referred to the huge building project that she had been involved with, stating,

> The situation I found in that parish, it was obvious that there were only two choices: sink or swim. So focus was both something I had but it was also a necessity. I think if I hadn't had it we would have just closed the parish down.

She went on to say,

> By the time I'd been in post six months it was apparent that the structural problems were huge. I actually wrote down 'mad plan' as a title for a paper because I knew the church was going to have to be pulled down. It didn't have any long-term life. I had to have a strategic plan because either the parish closed on the council estate or we took it forward to something new. So we built an eight and a half, nine million pound project.

Matt scored 10 for Advantage and 7.6 for Creativity. And the way in which these two significant facets work together enabled him to spot potential opportunities in the interface between taking services for the local community and discovering that his church building required expensive repairs. This is apparent in the following response:

> So, for example, having things like the Remembrance Day service or the miners' memorial service, or the miners' gala service with banners, coming together with having a quinquennial inspection that says, 'Your roof's shot and you need a hundred thousand pounds to put the building back together again.' It's seeing the synergies of those two events and thinking, 'Oh, actually these are linked.' Because, clearly, one of the things that the church does for the community is to form a rallying point for a sense of community identity and a piece of shared history. And so you suddenly see a link between those two and then you think, 'Well, repairing the church, or at least making public the church's need and trying to rally the community in general around the church's need, is a way of making the connections here, and getting the community to perhaps reassess its relationship with the church.' You're forcing the community to say, 'Actually, we want you to be here.' So, the creativity isn't in thinking something utterly out of the ether, it's in making connections.

Jim outlined various building-related issues with which he was dealing but went on to say that he felt that these things were not unusual for clergy. Since he scored 9.2 in Creativity, I asked him if he saw potential for new ways of doing things in the midst of dealing with challenging building issues. His positive response was enthusiastic, and he talked about things being 'God given', and also the role of networking and 'firing things off each other'. The problems with the building had prompted deeper engagement with the congregation; Jim gave the example of working with his family-service planning group, in which he felt there was a lot of creativity and from which he got a lot of energy:

> One of the ideas was nativity figures travelling round the community. The group came up with some fantastic ideas around that and it generated such a buzz and so much energy around the young folks. And these ideas transferred to a big community event. Sowing a few seeds and creating space and giving encouragement to people enabled those exciting ideas to be generated. So, as a leader I'm being creative there, but actually those ideas are coming from a wider set of people. And as Christians we believe that when we gather the Holy Spirit is there, so that God's hand is in that as well.

Jim felt that dealing with building-related issues was part and parcel of the ordained minister's task, and that his creativity was enabling him to focus on generating energy for outward-looking activities from within his planning group rather than on problems with the building.

With very few exceptions, ordained ministers in all the mainstream denominations will find themselves responsible for the care and maintenance of a church building or buildings. Buildings are a resource, but their care and maintenance, particularly if they are listed, can become burdensome and can detract from other aspects of ministry and mission. The responses of the ministers who spoke about church buildings nevertheless implied a positive attitude to a building-based ministry rather than resentment, resignation or negativity. While acknowledging the challenges and difficulties of spending time and effort on resolving the building-related issues with which they found themselves confronted, these ministers had been able to identify inherent opportunities. And, while Matt was still discerning a way forward, others had responded creatively and innovatively, acting in order to see recognizable social and spiritual capital generated.

The interview responses made it clear that this was not achieved by any of the ministers working alone, but rather alongside others, and the ministers who spoke about buildings all scored highly on their Team facet.[1] Bolton and Thompson tell us that

---

[1] Rupert and Susan, neither of whom mentioned issues with buildings specifically, achieved Team scores of 10 and 8 respectively. The average score for Team for the seven ordained ministers was 9.4.

When the Team facet is strong the social capital will be within the team, producing a high level of mutual trust and a common purpose. The [initiative] will move forward at a rate that the entrepreneur could never achieve alone. When problems arise they will be shared.[2]

For these ministers, the problems thrown up by church buildings in need of closure, repair or rebuilding were shared with others. For Dan and Roger, these 'others' were members of the teams they had put together. Matt was eager to assemble teams, while Jim worked with a planning group, although he did not use the language of teams. Jane too worked extensively with others, although she did not speak of teams in any of her responses.

The variety of ways in which the respondents worked with others is considered in the following chapter. And we may hope that, while a variety of challenging building-related issues are bound to demand time and attention from ordained and lay ministers in all denominations in the coming decades, the entrepreneurial minister will see in these the opportunity for creative and innovative solutions that have the potential to make a positive impact on the wider community.

---

[2] Bill Bolton and John Thompson, *The Entrepreneur in Focus: Achieve Your Potential* (London: Thompson Learning, 2003), 130.

7

Teamwork and partnering with others

Each of the interview respondents spoke about working with (rather than working *for*) their congregations. In addition Roger, Rupert and Dan also spoke about working with other clergy, although only Jane and Susan spoke directly about working with bodies external to the Church.

When a priest is ordained in the Church of England, the Preface, read out at the beginning of the ordination service, states that it is the task of the priest to 'lead God's people in the offering of praise and the proclamation of the gospel'.[1] Although the Preface is clear that 'In baptism the whole Church is summoned to witness to God's love and to work for the coming of his kingdom',[2] its emphasis does not imply that the priest should build teams but rather that all those within the Church should recognize the part that they must play in collaborating with the coming kingdom of God. Indeed, it is possible to interpret the words 'to lead' in a variety of ways, some of which would not take into account the possibility of teams at all.

Taken in its entirety, the Preface sets out a ministry that is designed to build up and sustain the people of God in lives of worship. It is only in recent decades that ordained and lay people in some parts of the Church of England have made a connection between the task set out for the priest in the Preface and its achievement by encouraging the building and sustaining of teams within congregations. Although it is overly simplistic to divide the presence of teams in church along lines of churchmanship, it is interesting to note that, of the seven ordained ministers whose responses are analysed here, the four who described themselves as evangelical (Roger, Matt, Rupert and Dan)

---

[1] From *Common Worship: Ordination Services* (London: Church House Publishing, 2007), 32.
[2] From *Common Worship: Ordination Services*, 32.

gave evidence of encouraging teams as part of their ministry. Of the three who described themselves as Anglo-Catholic (Jane, Susan and Jim), two did not mention teams at all; the other (Susan) only mentioned teams once, and this was in the context of wanting to enable teams rather than deliberately build them.

Having said this, Jane and Susan both articulated high levels of collaboration with their local communities and placed enormous emphasis on creating partnerships with bodies external to the church, and Jim adopted a highly collaborative approach with his congregations and was the only priest to mention specifically the importance of networking. Moreover, of the four evangelical priests whose responses included references to teams, further exploration suggested that only two were involved with teams that appeared to be healthy and flourishing.

I should say that I am not making a value judgement in relation to the presence of teams within churches. I have made it clear that the Preface does not explicitly require priests to build teams but rather that team building is an approach adopted by parts of the Church in response to a particular understanding of the role of the ordained minister and as one way of fulfilling what appears to be required by the Preface. Over the past several decades the mainstream denominations have grown more familiar with language drawn from the world of business and although, as discussed in Chapter 1, some continue to have an issue with the language around entrepreneurship, many churches appear to have less of a problem embracing language around 'team'.

We might observe that Dan, Rupert, Jim and Matt each had commercial careers prior to ordination, and Susan (although making only minor reference to teams) spent more than a decade working in education. Team working is standard practice in many areas of business and in education. Jim did not mention teams but his responses included a positive account of working closely and fruitfully with the family-service planning group. In contrast, Roger and Jane had always worked for the Church in some capacity but in spite of this, Roger's comments about the presence of a team of volunteers in his congregation implied a taken-for-granted attitude. My point here is that although all of the respondents commented on working with others, it is possible from their responses to discern differences in who those 'others' are, a range of reasons for working with others, a variety of approaches to working with them and a variation in levels of collaboration and power-sharing.

As mentioned above, only two respondents, Dan and Roger, made any significant comment about working with teams in their own congregations, although Rupert discussed building a team of clergy in the deanery as part of his role as area dean. Dan, who had previously worked in finance, talked at length about the four 'Ministry Development Teams' whose emergence he had overseen in his congregation. The teams covered youth, pastoral care, administration and mission, and they advised the church council. The congregation nominated individuals who expressed a developing sense of vocation and team members were then selected by Dan, the area dean and the archdeacon. Dan had taken the lead on this process but, according to him, the result had been a highly collaborative ministry in which others appeared to have a genuine influence in the life of the church.

Dan is an example of an ordained entrepreneurial minister whose ability to work with others, and specifically to create and sustain functional teams, had the effect of multiplying the impact of his entrepreneurial approach to ordained ministry. He said,

> I am a team member and a team player. I've worked very hard, and one of the best things I've done here is build a very committed team of people who have discovered their own vocation. I think this is what team building in churches is really all about. It's about trying to enable people to see that they've got a role and a ministry to fulfil in their own right with their own name on it, and the church has flourished as a result of it.

He went on to discuss the nature of the teams and the effect that he believed they were having, and he hinted at the fact that moving into a team mode was not straightforward for the church:

> It took some time to reorientate the church in that direction because this approach isn't run by agendas and minutes. It's based on prayer and Bible study, fellowship, relationships that are based on trust, pastoral concerns for the church and vision, and in a parish like this I'd be the only person running the show but now we do it collaboratively. It's a team where we are seeing people emerging into leadership; into readership and ordained ministry. It's a marvellous thing that happens right in the very core of the church.

The level of influence that Dan claimed team members were able to have in his church was not echoed in the responses of the other six respondents. The closest discernible model was Roger, who had also encouraged a team – although not on the same scale as Dan, who said,

> These weren't going to be the vicar's little helpers. They were going to be people who were going to have a significant contribution to make to the direction of this church. Me and the congregation were going to be willing to allow the church to be shaped by them and not just by me and that's what's happened here and it's been a fantastic thing to be a part of, and I have a role within it.

In fact Dan was the only respondent whose comments pointed to a genuine sharing of power and influence within the congregation. In this context it appeared that the teams allowed for a structured sharing of power; this had resulted in an increase in the number of people becoming passionate about the mission of the church, had been a catalyst for the emergence of members of the congregation into lay and ordained leadership, and had contributed to the numerical growth of the church. It had also shaped the way in which Dan understood his ministry: 'And my role has changed because of it. I've become almost a sort of facilitator, enabler. My role has changed significantly in all sorts of ways.'

Roger spoke of 'a great team of volunteers' within his congregation and talked of being 'accountable to a team in leadership'. However, he admitted to having a tendency to become distracted by other things that interested him. We see this in his comment,

> I'm not a good finisher and I am quite a good grasshopper, in terms of flitting from one thing to the next. The challenge for me is that because there are always more things to be giving time to in parish ministry, it means that I fall prey to, at worst, choosing just what I fancy, rather than what is important or urgent.

Having a team in place meant that the various strands of the church operation did not collapse when Roger became interested in other church-related projects. Roger's responses included the following admission: 'I'm conscious that sometimes people get pretty close to burnout and on reflection I wasn't there for them. I think that's because I've got too much of my own agenda going on to stay with the team-enabling role.'

Although the data does not allow me to comment on each respondent's deeper motivation, I suggest that, taken in their entirety, Roger's responses indicate that here was a minister whose entrepreneurial nature manifested itself in a habitual interest in a range of personally engaging projects, some of which he subsequently found it difficult to follow through on. However, his entrepreneurial nature had also led him to recognize the importance of a team of volunteers, because this meant that while he gave his attention to a range of initiatives, the activity of the volunteers ensured that the church continued to function. From his responses it appeared that rather than genuinely sharing power in the church and working towards collaborative leadership of the sort outlined by Dan, Roger might have been using the word 'team' to refer to simply being amenable to having members of his congregation take responsibility for some of the tasks that required attention and to ensure that he did not leave things unfinished. He said, 'I thrive with having co-leaders and shared responsibility. As it happens one of my church wardens is such a finisher so that's my salvation, being accountable to her.'

He stated that he was involved in shared ministry but also admitted that the power and influence lay with him: 'We have a massive commitment to being a shared ministry parish. Having said that, my ministry development team continue to look to me to be the prime envisioner, really.'

He did go on to say that the movement was away from him as prime visionary: 'That's changing. I think of one person in particular who is getting really good at completely outside the box ideas.' But even here it appeared that rather than being a move towards something comparable with the sort of team situation outlined by Dan, the reality was closer to a willingness to encourage individuals to share ideas, a preparedness to allow those with enthusiasm to join in and relief that the church warden was prepared to hold him to account and act as a finisher.

Rupert looked after five parishes and was also area dean. He commented only briefly on working with his congregations, and this was to express a sense of frustration. The deanery was the primary focus for his reflections on working with others, which was unsurprising given that he described himself (as did Jane) as a 'big-picture person' and claimed to spend more than half of his time on the deanery.

Rupert's interview responses suggested that he had adopted a highly collaborative approach in his previous career, and this had continued in his ordained ministry:

> I always valued and took teams for granted and the longest spell of my commercial career was with a large, multinational corporation but it wasn't very hierarchical. Lots of things had to happen through persuasion and the force of argument and good ideas.

And in relation to his ordained ministry he said, 'I take it for granted that you work across the streams and across the denominations. You do unless you can't.'

His comments on teamwork were focused on the way in which he worked with the deanery clergy:

> As area dean I've worked on trying to turn the clergy in the deanery into a real team where we actually pull together and support each other in practice in more than token ways, because we realize that there's so few of us that working collaboratively is good for all of us and good for all of our parishes and good for the mission of the Church.

Rupert made reference to his previous commercial career throughout his responses. He made a number of comparisons between his experience of working with others in business, which he talked about in very positive terms, and his experience of working with others in the church, which he expressed a good deal of frustration about. For example, he said,

> In industry I was able to pick my team. It's just not like that in the Church. You don't get to pick your team. You're into lay ministry. They're there. OK, you may draw more people in and you may develop people but it can be a very long haul. Their understanding of the organization is completely different, and of its purpose and goals. And yes, I do believe in a simple ministry of presence, that's lovely, but you need a few people to be present, don't you?

These comments were made in the context of responding to a question about the sorts of things that hinder the exercise of entrepreneurship in the parish. Rupert talked about the continuing negative impact of his predecessor's belief that it was not possible for the five parishes of which he had oversight to work together as a collaborative group. Rupert had spent several years working towards achieving what his predecessor had believed was impossible and felt that he had made real progress. However, he commented, 'This is the hardest thing I've ever done, by a long way.' He claimed that he naturally worked in teams and sought to do so as a result of having highly positive experiences of teamwork in his previous career in industry. He expressed frustration at working with others in the Church and explained that people there had a completely different understanding of how the organization works.

It was possible that it was this frustration that led him to focus his natural desire to work collaboratively on building a sense of team with the clergy of his deanery. With this group he was able to shape and influence the direction of the team. In his estimation the result was positive. He said, 'Our deanery is going for an innovative deanery plan in the most obvious and determined way. That is partly a reflection of my approach; a longer-term, more change-orientated view of things.'

Interestingly, in terms of working with members of the congregation across his five parishes, he referenced the archdeacon's emphasis on having a recognized pastor in each community. But he then flipped this around and made a highly innovative proposal:

> I could manage the pastoral stuff if I had an entrepreneur in every parish. They don't need to be ordained, they don't need to be a lay reader. They might need some theological training and some equipping. But right now I think I would kill for an entrepreneur in every one of my parishes; a recognized entrepreneur.

He expanded on this radical proposal and provided a plausible rationale, saying:

> Community entrepreneurship rests on having the existing networks and as an incomer you don't have the existing network. I'm starting to think, who are the people who could be my entrepreneur in that village? The people I can trust and say, 'Yeah, innovate here. Come and tell me what you want to do and we'll talk about it and, yes, let's go for it.' They are rooted in the community and will have the respect and trust and will be able to take some of those things forward or to gather other people around them. Being an entrepreneur on your own is pretty blooming lonely. I couldn't do that. I can pastor them, I can care for them, I can provide a framework.

This innovative response to the issue of offering ministry to five congregations and engaging in mission across five communities would involve Rupert in a significant sharing of power and influence.

This was something he appeared to be comfortable with. In fact, he concluded his interview by lamenting the fact that as clergy numbers were reduced and parishes brought together in increasingly large groups, power was moving away from the local and becoming more distant. His suggestion of establishing a recognized entrepreneur in each community is in line with the view, taken in this book, that the exercise of entrepreneurship in the local church by both ordained and lay ministers should be widely encouraged. Putting the suggestion into action would, like many entrepreneurial ventures, involve some degree of risk. However, it is a possibility that warrants further exploration because it appears to hold potential for reversing the movement of power away from local or parish level and returning it to people with close ties to their communities and who have the knowledge, networks and trust to engage in faithful and transforming ministries.

In Rupert's responses, it was interesting to note the frustration present in the repeated comparison of his highly positive experience of working collaboratively in business with his very different experience of attempting to work with others in the Church. In contrast, frustration was absent from Susan's and Jane's comments about working with others in their congregations and communities. Unlike Dan and Rupert, Susan and Jane did not have previous experience in business with which to compare working with people in parish ministry. And although Susan had worked in education, she did not hold a position that allowed her to exercise strategic influence in terms of forming teams.

Both Susan and Jane (with Social scores of 9 and 9.6 respectively) articulated something about their motivation for ministry in the interview and made a direct connection between love and working with others by engaging with the wider community. In relation to her motivation in parish ministry, Susan remarked, 'The church is here to serve the community so I start by loving and living the community. I am driven by wanting the church and the community to know that God loves them.'

On the same issue Jane claimed that 'We are motivated by our love of Christ to engage with our community.' As ordained ministers who spoke positively about working with others, Rupert and Dan may well have had similar motivations, but these were not articulated in their interview responses. Although Jane and Susan were both focused, driven and motivated, neither spoke of being frustrated with any aspect of working with their congregations or communities. In fact, both spoke frankly about the neediness of those with whom they were working, and their responses implied that enabling and encouraging others over time, without a particular set of expectations other than actively sharing God's love, was part of what they each understood to be the task of the ordained minister.

From their responses, Jane and Susan – who both located themselves in the Anglo-Catholic tradition – appeared to be working from an understanding of ordained ministry that was comfortable with the minister leading 'from the front' on behalf of those for whom he or she was pastorally responsible. These 'others' included the local community as well as the congregation. Both Jane's and Susan's narratives indicated that theirs were enabling ministries focused on encouraging and building up the self-esteem and self-confidence of those within their congregations and on acts of loving service to those outside the church.

Both ministers were working in socially challenging areas with congregations and communities comprised of those who were, on the whole, less educated and less skilled than either of them. For example, Jane said, 'We are talking about council estates and those people are, at best, blue collar workers.' And from their responses, Susan and Jane both appeared to embody an autonomous model of ordained ministry and church leadership; that is, neither was working as part of a ministry team within their churches, although both encouraged high levels of congregational participation. From their responses it appeared that power in the church and in the engagement of the church with the local community remained with Jane and Susan as priests and that both were exercising wide-ranging, albeit apparently positive influence, as a result of their encouragement of congregation members and the energy they put into working with bodies outside the church. Both Susan and Jane talked about partnership with the local authorities, although Jane's partnership experience was significantly greater than Susan's due to the rebuilding project in which she had taken the lead role.

Of all the respondents, Jane was the most extensively involved in partnerships with external bodies, and it was here that her entrepreneurial drive and ability were most apparent. From her responses, Jane's ministry could be described as one of spending significant time and energy on creating partnerships with external bodies to create financial and social capital that was beneficial to the church and the local community; this, alongside encouraging, building up and organizing individuals within the congregation, appeared to be a source of deep satisfaction and fulfilment for her personally.

In relation to creating partnerships with outside bodies, Jane explained: 'I know what people will fund. I know what rings their bell.' She went on to say that in partnership, 'you have to see the idea that will work', adding that 'You can tick the local authority boxes and they will give you money.' She pointed out that in the local church, 'It is easy to have the same people doing the same things', and she spoke about the importance of recognizing skills within the congregation, saying that 'The sort of people I asked to assist with leading worship raised eyebrows but their confidence grew.' She went on to express her opinion that 'An important part of the ordained minister's job is enabling damaged people to become who God created them to be.'

Susan said she worked naturally with others and spoke of aiming to enable teams, although in her examples she only alluded to particular individuals or existing groups and the way in which she aimed to encourage them or build up their self-esteem. Like Jane, however, Susan's entrepreneurial ability and drive were most evident in the way she spoke extensively about working with outside bodies, particularly the local authority, on specific, community-related initiatives. Susan was not setting out to create teams but rather appeared to be attempting to leverage her influence as the ordained minister and to maximize the potential of her ministry and the ministry of the Church in the local community. She talked about 'walking beside people' to give them confidence and about helping people to know that God loves them by 'loving, trusting and valuing' them. She was clear that it was 'about asking who all this is for'. She talked about using 'we' instead of 'I' and mentioned being content for everything not to be 'perfect' in order to allow the congregation to join in. She talked about finding 'fun and creative ways to express passion' and said that this might be a chore but that things might emerge. She explained that even if she didn't see the growth she was content to keep doing things, 'so that people know that God loves them'.

Like Susan and Jane, Matt, previously a chief executive, appeared to be leading from the front but spoke of being keen to create teams of 'critical individuals'. From the overall shape of Matt's responses, the extent to which these teams would ultimately share the vision and the leadership was not clear. Matt talked about being hurt by the way in which the church council refused to support a particular change that he felt was necessary. In response he explained that he thought the following (though he did not say this to the church council):

> Right! I'll do it without you then. I need to do this. This needs to happen, mission will fail if we don't do this so if you won't help me I'll have to go and find somebody else to help me.

The sentiment contained in this comment is what one might typically expect from an entrepreneur. But it provokes serious reflection in the context of local church ministry, since one might argue that in order for anything of lasting impact to occur in a local church, a minister will need to gain the support of the church leadership at some point. In fact, if something of kingdom value is going to have a chance of emerging, then this will need to come from *within* the congregation or the wider community rather than being an idea of vision imposed by the ordained minister. Instead the ordained minister will act as facilitator and midwife as the process of bringing something new to birth goes through its various stages.

Matt spoke a good deal about the importance of articulating vision and building up trust within the congregation, but the above comment pointed to the possibility that his personal sense of the direction in which the church should be heading and his determination to achieve this would be the dominant drivers. He appeared to be willing to work with the church council, but only in so far as they were willing to lend support to his vision. When this failed he talked about working around them by finding others to help him. In his response he talked about creating teams, saying,

> One of the things I feel I absolutely must create, otherwise I will feel I've failed, is a team or teams. I will not have succeeded if I don't create teams. I may not yet know them. In fact, I have a strong suspicion I don't yet know them. Otherwise, whatever else I achieve, it won't be what I want and it won't be sustainable and it won't be anywhere near the right kind of satisfying outcome for me.

From Matt's responses it is possible to infer that he imagined that a team or teams might help him to achieve what the church council would not. The existence of teams would also give him a personal sense of satisfaction and fulfilment. It is not clear that Matt would encourage or enable the teams to generate their own sense of vision. In fact, from the comments he made in relation to the church council, we might infer that teams would ultimately be a vehicle for achieving Matt's vision for the church in spite of the church council rather than becoming an opportunity for genuinely collaborative ministry and the sharing of power and influence. It is interesting that he said,

> I thought as an entrepreneur I was being almost the antithesis of the team builder, you know, almost the person who causes a real tension in the team, an absolute pain in the bum. That's been my model of entrepreneur and I think well, actually, that doesn't describe me. I am someone who will tend to wait for the others to catch up with me. Not that I'm going to stop on the journey but I want people with me.

In the context of this particular local church, and in spite of the comments he made about not being the kind of entrepreneur who would 'cause real tension in a team', we might conclude from his responses – including the admission that he will 'wait for others to catch up' rather than giving them any genuine say in where they are going, and that he isn't going to 'stop on the journey' – that the particular shape of Matt's entrepreneurial nature would make it difficult for him to form and sustain the types of teams he talked about and the types of team that would flourish in the context of the church in which he is ministering. And indeed he went on to say,

> My preferred mode of operation is to gather people and be part of the team. I guess if I'm really honest, my really preferred mode is to lead teams. There we go. It sounds a bit egotistical, but that's that. That's when I'm at my best.

Various negative factors emerged from the analysis of the respondents' comments on partnering and working with others. Roger admitted that team members had come close to burnout while he was involved in other initiatives. Matt had been hurt by the church council's refusal to support his ideas and was intending to build a team in order to achieve his vision in spite of them. Rupert expressed a sense of frustration at the time and energy taken to work with congregations on collaboration. None of the ministers, moreover, with the exception of Dan and Rupert, expressed a desire to move towards a situation in which power and influence was more obviously or directly shared with the congregation; a detail that, in the context of Christian ministry in the way of Jesus, must provoke prayerful self-examination and honest reflection.

But a number of positive effects also emerged from these comments. These were effects that respondents felt were the result of ministering in a collaborative way, and they included:

1 encouraging and energizing the ordained minister and the congregation;
2 building up faith within the congregation;
3 building up self-worth and self-confidence in the members of the congregation;
4 encouraging and enabling leadership to emerge within the congregation;
5 making contact and building positive relationships with the local community;
6 discerning the needs of the local community;
7 generating mutually beneficial relationships with external bodies such as the local authority;
8 generating revenue through partnerships with external bodies;
9 meeting the needs of the local community and local institutions such as schools.

The participants' responses, particularly those that are less than positive, along with my own experience of working with lay and ordained ministers and congregations, lead me to suggest that it does not go without saying that ministers will naturally and effectively partner and work with others, whether via simple collaboration with individuals, team-building or partnering with bodies outside the church. The comments of Jane, Susan, Rupert, Jim and Dan in relation to working with others nevertheless suggest that as they have focused attention on spending time with their congregations (as well as outside agencies, in the cases of Jane and Susan), and as they have listened and attempted to encourage and enable people, it has become possible for ideas to emerge, for trust to be built and for energy to be released in the minister, the congregation and the local community. It appears from the responses that such energy can become a driver for a range of spiritually and socially beneficial initiatives. The responses of Rupert, Susan, Jane and Dan, meanwhile, suggest that when ministers work in a genuinely collaborative or team-focused way with their congregations, they need to have the courage to acknowledge that things may not be done in the way they might prefer, and the grace to cope both with the resulting diversions from their vision and the accompanying personal frustrations.

Dan's responses, which involved considered reflection on the building up and maintenance of teams in his church, included the observation that leaders had emerged as a result of involvement in team ministry. Providing an opportunity for church members to participate in teams in which they can take on genuine responsibility, grow in confidence and see the effect of their labours on the life of the church and the wider community is clearly positive. Dan claimed that his church had grown numerically since his arrival, although we cannot conclude from this that there is necessarily a direct correlation between the presence of teams and the growth of the church congregation. This is an area where further research would be useful. Jane and Susan also claimed that their congregations had experienced limited growth, and their responses lead me to suggest that working in partnership with local authorities and other bodies has the potential to generate previously unseen opportunities as well as revenue for the church, while providing services for local people and breaking down perceived barriers to church in the minds of the local community.

8

What factors help entrepreneurship to happen?

When asked about what he felt would aid the exercise of entrepreneurship in his situation as a minister, Roger responded by talking about the need to strengthen and renew faith in congregations and said that he felt that if this happened it would equip people to be entrepreneurs within congregations. He said,

> We've got to believe that God is going to make a massive difference and that he'll be generous enough to involve us in that process, and I think that is a matter of strengthening our faith in a dynamic God.

Roger and Susan, however, were the only respondents to mention God or faith in God in relation to this question. Matt's response focused on building vision and trust. He talked about the need for the ordained minister to articulate a compelling vision that captivated rather than obliged, and expanded on how important he felt it was to develop trust:

> Entrepreneurship inevitably entails taking people where they have not been before and people won't go where they haven't been before unless they trust you, which is why just being a task-orientated, purpose-driven person isn't going to work in church – because people pick that up straight away and run a mile from you. You've got to be interested enough in them as them, listening as well as talking and proving that you care. If you don't do that enough, quite simply they won't trust you, and if they don't trust you it ain't gonna happen.

Jane made several responses in rapid succession, citing the need for accessible language, looking at how clergy are trained, emphasizing the importance of focus and asking what the goals are and where the strategy is. It was not clear from her response whether it was the ordained minister, the congregation or the wider Church who should be asking themselves about goals and strategy. Jane explained that she felt that a lot of clergy would never be naturally entrepreneurial, but said:

> If you want an entrepreneurial spirit within the church, you might find ways to enable them to recognize it's not their gift rather than forcing them to think that they should be like that, or to enable them to reach the level of ability. And if it's not beyond a certain point, having people who will help a church generate that entrepreneurial spirit like consultants.

But Jane went on to lament the fact that despite her extensive experience of involvement in partnerships, rebuilding and regeneration in her previous diocese, neither that diocese nor her current one had invited her to share her expertise. She suggested that the scale of what she had been involved with, and had ultimately achieved, had made her previous bishop uncomfortable and said that he didn't seem to know what to do with her. In relation to this she said, 'I don't really think the Church really wants entrepreneurs. Nobody ever thought, "Well, we should be having a conversation with these people." No one ever did. And to this day doesn't.'

She expanded on the way in which her entrepreneurial nature continued to drive her to work at making connections in order to generate revenue for the church, saying, 'I've just put a bid in for Diamond Jubilee money. If I tick the boxes I get the money and I can do things. Without that money I can't do it because our budget doesn't allow.'

Building on her previous positive experiences of working with others, and drawing on the tenacity and boldness that are part of her entrepreneurial nature, Jane reflected on both the process and the fruit of her efforts:

> You've got to go out and wheel and deal. And my folks know I do it. Some of them won't approve, because I'm not a traditional parish priest, but we've had farmers' markets in the church with over a thousand people through the doors in a building they've never been in even though they've lived in the town. People are becoming familiar with the building and they are living in the space. So when they need us for their baptisms, for the funerals, this is a familiar space.

She went on to talk about recognizing a quality in herself that is central to effective entrepreneurship: the ability to see something through to completion. Bolton and Thompson discuss this in relation to 'building something of recognized value'. Jane said,

> In some respects I'm horribly conventional. I'm an old-fashioned Anglo-Catholic priest, but I also recognize that in my skills base I'm not an ordinary parish priest because I have done *extra* ordinary things. Not extraordinary but *extra* ordinary things. And I've seen it through. Someone who wrote a reference for me said that 'you get the visionary and the closer, someone that can actually have the vision and deliver and see it to the end'. We will dream the dreams but we will also have the reality.

Rupert talked about the need for generating a permission-giving culture, from the bishop downwards. He spoke of this in relation to perceived boundaries, mentioning canon law as an example which, he said, could feel like a straitjacket to many – although he added that for some it seemed that the perceived boundaries were a 'comforting straitjacket'.

In her response to this question, Susan talked about the gift of the dog collar, which, she said, 'enables us to get into places and into people's lives and into a group, a community where we've never set foot before and where we're more or less accepted and respected'.

She also mentioned the fact that ordained ministers do not have someone 'looking over their shoulder'. She explained that this meant there was freedom for the minister to harness his or her particular passion and 'use the motivation to turn those opportunities and those doors that might be opened by the collar into real chances to make a difference in that place'.

She discussed the importance, in her view, of ordained ministers being themselves in a parish and explained that she felt that the Church of England was good at encouraging priests to minister within a parish as the person they were:

> The Church of England respects the fact that God calls us to be each day more fully who we are, not to be somebody completely different. And I think the church does try to honour that. And I think if you've got a very unfortunate bishop or archdeacon, that's hard and you have to find a creative way round that. But where people are going to thrive as entrepreneurs, its where they're respected for who they are and allowed to be who they are with a huge amount of freedom within a context to go and build the kingdom.

Like Matt, Susan mentioned the importance of trust, but rather than talking about gaining the trust of the congregation in order that they should feel able to buy into the vision articulated by the ordained minister, she talked about the priest trusting the congregation:

> We have to see ourselves as part of that community and then lead in with absolute integrity and be led by them with absolute integrity and trust in them. That's where people are going to flourish, and that's where we're going to see real skills and real entrepreneurship, and I think real growth and excitement.

Jim talked about the importance of having a focus on others rather than on yourself and gaining an understanding of the context. Related to this was the importance for the ordained minister of being informed what the issues in the parish are and being provided with tools that help to develop an understanding of the issues for the church and community. He also discussed the importance of continuing mental stimulation for the minister, giving the personal example of pursuing a part-time course of study for a master's degree. He mentioned the importance that he placed on networks and networking for generating and realizing ideas. Finally, he talked about the need for shared vision, although he admitted that, since he had only been in his current ministerial position for a short time, he had not achieved this yet. He explained that it was important to have 'Good vision and a shared understanding of what the *raison d'être* of the church is in that place and what the mission of the church is in that place.'

In summary, from the interview responses I identified 19 factors that the respondents felt aided the exercise of entrepreneurship in their ministry. These factors (not presented in any particular order) are:

1 strengthening the faith of those in the church;
2 creating a vision shared by lay and ordained ministers and the congregation;
3 building mutual trust between lay and ordained ministers and the congregation;
4 using accessible language;
5 ongoing attention to the selection, training and deployment of clergy with a view to ensuring that candidates with entrepreneurial ability are encouraged and supported;

6 being able to focus;
7 being clear about goals;
8 being clear about strategy;
9 using consultants to help churches to generate an entrepreneurial spirit;
10 wider church structures, ensuring that entrepreneurial expertise is shared;
11 having the courage to go beyond the church, to experiment and look for opportunities;
12 lay and ordained ministers being both visionary *and* closer;
13 creating a permission-giving culture at every level in the church;
14 ordained ministers utilizing their recognized status within the local community (the dog collar is a resource);
15 encouraging lay and ordained entrepreneurial ministers to be themselves and to minister out of their entrepreneurial nature;
16 the local church maintaining a focus on others rather than on themselves;
17 ordained and lay ministers understanding their context and the particular issues being faced by those in their local community;
18 providing local churches with tools to aid such understanding;
19 building networks and engaging in networking with the intention of generating and realizing appropriate ideas.

One helpful way to imagine how these factors could potentially hang together in practice is to connect and present them in the form of a narrative. Such a narrative might appear as follows:

As churches in the UK engage with the complex realities of the current mission task, the various denominations increasingly recognize and address the need to select, train and deploy ministers who are able to engage in entrepreneurial approaches to ministry in their local church, or to encourage and support others in adopting an entrepreneurial approach. As a result, lay and ordained ministers emerge who prioritize the strengthening of their own faith in God and that of their congregations. These ministers are cultivators of a rich environment for growth. They communicate effectively and apply themselves to generating trust and, as a result, shared visions for new growth and outreach emerge in congregations. Where appropriate and necessary, the shared vision is stimulated by the involvement of entrepreneurial consultants working alongside local churches. The shared vision emerges organically and is characterized by focus and by clarity in relation to goals and strategy. All those in the church maintain a keen awareness of people beyond the church, and they use appropriate resources to discern the needs of the local community. The members of the church have the courage to experiment with opportunities beyond their walls and when projects are undertaken they are completed. Ideas and energy for ordained ministers and congregations are stimulated and realized through networks and networking. This process is helped by the existence of a permission-giving culture in the local, regional and national church. Such a culture encourages lay and ordained entrepreneurial ministers to embrace an entrepreneurial approach to ministry in line with their natural gifts and competencies. Entrepreneurial expertise is shared between local churches and this, in turn, underpins the culture of permission and stimulates further entrepreneurial ministry.

Since a number of respondents contributed to the list, these factors don't function as a comprehensive approach to be undertaken by any one entrepreneurial minister. They were drawn from responses to interview questions rather than from observations, and this means we cannot ascertain what relation the factors suggested by each minister bear to the reality of that person's ministry. Nor do the interview responses allow me to comment on whether and to what extent putting the factors into practice would make an entrepreneurial approach to ministry more possible, or to assert that doing so would result in particular outcomes such as spiritual or numerical growth, more effective loving service to the local community or the generation of social or financial capital. A church reflecting on the factors mentioned here with the intention of considering how to encourage a more entrepreneurial approach to ministry should also reflect on the content of the following chapter, in which I consider factors that might hinder the exercise of entrepreneurship.

9

What hinders entrepreneurship?

When asked about the factors that might hinder the exercise of entrepreneurship in the parish, Roger responded with a qualified insight that was particularly helpful in the context of pastoral ministry: 'I think the sheer weight of the bread and butter stuff can be a hindrance. And yet, we need to find the perceived opportunities in the bread and butter stuff.' He went on to admit that this was a demanding balancing act, but claimed that entrepreneurial ministers would have an advantage in achieving it.

Matt said that he felt entrepreneurship was not part of the corporate ethos of the Church of England or any of the mainstream denominations, and this made it difficult for entrepreneurship to flourish:

> Care, spirituality, however that's interpreted, pastoral concern, respect for tradition, all that kind of thing, they're deep in the Anglican ethos. But entrepreneurship isn't and if you're an entrepreneur and, boy am I an entrepreneur, you pick that up.

He went on to talk about entrepreneurship being hindered as a result of the low demands made by the Church of England and the accompanying low levels of personal discipleship:

> The Church of England makes really, really low demands on people and that, in a way, is fantastic and in another way it's potentially fatal. When you come into a context and you see need and you see opportunity, you find you've got very low currency to deal with because the grounds on which people belong to church are thin. Frankly their personal belonging to Jesus is thin, so you've got not much to trade with. It is a bit like building bricks without straw.

Jane's immediate response to the question of what might hinder entrepreneurship in the parish was 'fear'. She did not expand on this, but went on to say that she felt that in the current situation of the Church, other factors were that ordained ministers could not have many dreams, were confused about what they were being asked to do, were being asked to do so many things that they felt disempowered or were the wrong person in the wrong place. She added that she felt that lots of ordained ministers simply could not be entrepreneurial, and said, 'If you want an entrepreneurial Church, that has to be taken into account in terms of how you select and train people and certainly how the bishops put certain people into certain parishes.'

Rupert felt that entrepreneurship was hindered by those who were loyal to the institution rather than to 'the cause or the gospel': 'The people who are entrepreneurial are the ones who are loyal to the cause and to the gospel more than they are to the system or to any party within the system.'

He went on to say that in a parish an unhelpful sense of history, meaning what was or was not done by the minister's predecessor, could hinder entrepreneurship. Picking up on themes mentioned by Matt and Jane, he also talked about an undervaluing of entrepreneurship in the Church of England:

> I think the qualities we bring as entrepreneurial clergy are not suf-
> ficiently valued in the Church of England. Many people find them
> irritating and annoying. I'm talking about senior people. I was in my
> forties when I was ordained and there is a general undervaluing of
> those skills that people like myself bring in from pre-ordination ex-
> perience, which is really, really distressing and difficult for a lot of us.

Like Rupert, Susan touched on the potential impact of senior leadership on entrepreneurship in the parish, but her response was pragmatic:

> There might be barriers with the bishop or the archdeacon or some-
> body who wants to micromanage, and that's where you might see
> people fail as entrepreneurs because that permission's not there or
> because there's a block. But I think true entrepreneurship says 'OK,
> that's a block there, either I have to persuade them, I have to demon-
> strate it in the way that I'm living and working or I simply have to find
> a way round this block.'

She talked about the impact that a difficult church council or leadership team could have on entrepreneurship, saying, 'A difficult PCC wouldn't shut entrepreneurship down but it would take an incredible amount of commitment and drive and energy and that in itself could become a factor which shuts it down.'

Susan's responses also included similar themes to Jane's. She mentioned entrepreneurship being hindered where clergy had low morale, or had forgotten why they were in the parish or were tired and lacking in motivation. She suggested that there was a continuing need for ordained ministers to consider their vocation, saying,

> This is the best job in the world if it's the right job. It might be about 'should I be a minister in *this* context?' Family, schooling might hold someone to a place but their job might be done there.

Jim's response to this question was brief. He cited lack of clarity, inward focus, poor relationships and lack of resource as factors that he felt hindered the exercise of entrepreneurship in his ministerial context.

In summary, from the interview responses I identified 22 factors that the ordained ministers felt hindered the exercise of entrepreneurship. The factors (not presented in any particular order) are:

1 the weight of the 'bread and butter stuff' (although opportunities may be perceived within this);
2 entrepreneurship not being part of the corporate ethos of the Church;
3 the low demands made by the Church of England;
4 low levels of personal discipleship;
5 fear;
6 ordained ministers being confused about their task;
7 ordained ministers being asked to do too many things;
8 ordained ministers feeling disempowered;
9 being the wrong minister in a particular parish;
10 those who are loyal to the institution rather than the gospel;
11 the presence of too many non-entrepreneurial layers in the Church;
12 the Church's undervaluing of entrepreneurial qualities and pre-ordination experience;
13 micromanagement;
14 a difficult church council;
15 ordained ministers having low morale;
16 ordained ministers losing a sense of purpose;
17 ordained ministers becoming tired;

18 ordained ministers losing motivation;
19 ordained ministers and congregations lacking clarity about their purpose;
20 an inward focus on the part of ordained ministers and/or the congregation;
21 poor relationships between ordained ministers and the congregation and/or within the congregation;
22 lack of resources to assist in understanding the issues affecting the local community.

As was the case in the previous chapter, each respondent contributed to the factors, so the above list does not reflect the view or experience of any one entrepreneurial minister. It is also worth pointing out that the factors listed are not necessarily correct or 'true' but are, rather, the perceptions of those interviewed; for example, it is the view of one respondent that entrepreneurship is not part of the corporate ethos of the Church of England. I am not suggesting that this is actually the case, but am reporting this response and presenting it for reflection.

Nor do the responses allow me to comment on whether and to what extent practically addressing the factors might make an entrepreneurial approach to ministry more possible or whether dealing with some or all of these factors would have the effect of making spiritual or numerical growth, service to the local community or the generation of social or financial capital more likely. A church wishing to encourage an entrepreneurial approach to ministry may find it helpful to reflect on the above factors alongside those set out in the previous chapter and to engage in a wide-ranging and frank discussion that includes ordained and lay ministers who demonstrate an entrepreneurial approach to ministry and mission. The themes presented above are not exhaustive but are simply those that emerged from the responses given to me by interview respondents. But I am able to say that, in the view of the respondents at the time of their interview, where one or more of these factors are present at some level in the ministers or the wider church, then an entrepreneurial approach to ministry may not flourish and may to some degree be hindered.

One omission from the list that I find surprising is the issue of buildings. Roger's comment about the weight of the 'bread and butter stuff' was the only response that could potentially be understood to embrace various building-related issues, but even here Roger was not specific. In considering the theme of buildings in Chapter 5, I noted that none of the respondents viewed dealing with building-related issues in a negative light. It is very interesting that when setting out factors that they felt could potentially hinder the exercise of entrepreneurship in their context, none of the ordained ministers mentioned church buildings. The various things mentioned were, in fact, all human factors and related either to the minister himself or herself, the congregation, the regional staff or the national church. In relation to the national church, although the perceived ethos of the institution was mentioned, the ethos of an institution is constructed, maintained and propagated by those within that institution, so that even here we are dealing with human factors rather than something static or inert, such as a building.

The factors have a cumulative effect: while individual factors may frustrate the potential exercise of an entrepreneurial approach to ministry, each will cause others, so it is likely that a number will be present and the effect of each on the potential for entrepreneurship will be multiplied. An example of the way in which this might occur, drawing on factors that might hinder the exercise of entrepreneurship, is as follows.

If, as claimed by one respondent, entrepreneurship is not part of the corporate ethos of a particular denomination, then this is likely to be evident at national, regional and local level and will take in every aspect of the life of the institution. I suggest that an absence of entrepreneurship in the ethos of a particular denomination may be evidenced by the following:

- a general suspicion of and resistance to change;
- defence of the status quo;
- limited and limiting relationships between congregations and leadership at local, regional and national level;
- limited connections between congregations and the wider community;

- limited evidence of growth in discipleship at congregational level;
- limited evidence of numerical growth, or, more likely, decline at congregational level;
- decline in clergy numbers;
- stagnating or dwindling finances.

Where we see evidence like this we may be led towards the view that entrepreneurship is not present: although an entrepreneurial approach to ministry is not a guarantee of numerical and financial growth, it is evidenced by factors which in most cases are the opposites of those just set out. Lack of entrepreneurship in the ethos of a particular denomination will also be evident in the way in which ordained ministers and others who are given leadership roles are selected, trained and deployed. Since employed staff, including ordained ministers, have a significant hand in shaping the life of the institutional churches, when selection, training and deployment does not deliberately seek to engage those with entrepreneurial ability or actively discourages the recruitment of individuals with such gifts, the net effect is likely to be the maintenance of a non-entrepreneurial ethos. And when this is the case, it may follow that the priorities of many within the institution are shaped more by loyalty to the institution and maintenance in its current form than by other areas of priority, especially those that involve some degree of change.

When this happens, as the surrounding culture changes and an accompanying need for (faithful and appropriate) change within the institution is not recognized or is resisted, the institution is likely to face declining numbers of participants and an accompanying decline in financial resources. As resources diminish and the institution moves towards the perception of looming crises, those with a vested interest in the system may perceive change as an ever greater risk, and therefore will be less likely to contemplate it or allow it to occur. Diminishing financial resources mean that clergy who leave or retire are less likely to be replaced. Tasks are divided up between fewer people who work harder, but for less obvious gains.

It is here that we are able to identify the sorts of factors that respondents felt hindered the exercise of entrepreneurship. Clergy involved in such a cycle may become afraid, confused, discouraged, tired and inwardly focused, and may lose a sense of purpose. Exhaustion and breakdown or a focus on moving on or retiring may follow. None of this is conducive to an entrepreneurial approach to ministry. The presence of each factor makes the others more likely and the possibility of entrepreneurship less so.

10

The impact of senior leadership on entrepreneurship in the local church

All of my respondents were ordained Anglicans working as parish priests. When I asked them to reflect on the extent to which entrepreneurship at local church level was affected by either the presence or the lack of entrepreneurship in the senior leadership, therefore, they understood that I was referring to the bishop and his senior staff team, which includes senior lay people, diocesan officers and archdeacons. Readers ministering in a different denomination will, I hope, be able to draw parallels with their own leadership structures and make appropriate comparisons with what I have set out in this chapter.

I found it interesting that all of the responses to questions about the impact of senior leadership on entrepreneurship at local level were relatively brief. Susan talked about the way in which a 'difficult' bishop or archdeacon could block entrepreneurship or simply not give permission for a particular project to go ahead. But she went on to talk about finding ways around this. Jane suggested that bishops who wanted to encourage an entrepreneurial church needed to think about the selection, training and deployment of clergy.

Dan felt that in his church there was scope for him to experiment and to re-imagine, and to give permission and encouragement to his congregation to do things. He also talked about being asked to take on an additional church, but pointed out that the stated intention of the senior staff was that this addition would be for growth rather than managing decline. Reflecting on this, he said,

> The structures have got to be eased a little bit in order that we can become the kind of church that making those changes will allow. Otherwise what you'll get if you're not careful is just overstretched, overtired clergy who can't do it because it's too much. We've got to try

and change the way we are in order to adapt to the circumstances that we're in today.

Dan felt that the structures were not serving the mission of the church and that adapting those structures needed to take account of the role of archdeacons:

> I just don't think that archdeacons are allowed to think beyond the structures. I think if they allowed themselves to see beyond their own structures we might see change and development happen in a more creative way than we're seeing right now. I just think that when we're talking about church development and mission we need a fresh conversation about what we're prepared to support and what we're not prepared to support. And this word, risk, is an interesting one coming from archdeacons. The greater risk is carrying on doing what you've always done.

In relation to the impact that an entrepreneurial bishop might have on ministry at local church level, Dan went on to say that 'We need resourcing and we need encouraging and we need inspiring leaders to help us to be inspired.'

Jim felt that the structure of the Church of England allowed ordained ministers to bury their heads in their parishes and not to be hugely affected by whether or not the senior leadership was entrepreneurial. In the context of Jim's other comments, I understood this to mean that ministers could get on with being entrepreneurial at local level without paying too much attention to what might be happening elsewhere in the diocese. Jim felt that 'sponsorship from the top' was necessary in order for initiatives at parish level to be more than simply 'islands' and to be sustainable once the ordained minister had moved on.

Rupert, as an area dean, described himself as 'middle management' and said that in this capacity he felt able to do a lot to encourage the clergy in his deanery to innovate and think differently. However, he felt that this could only go so far and that it helped if the senior leadership's mode of operation was entrepreneurial. Rupert too felt that non-entrepreneurial archdeacons could be a block to innovation. Reflecting on this, he said, 'If there are too many layers in the organization that are non-entrepreneurial, then it's like a fire-blanket which deadens everything. One, you can probably work through that, or even a couple.' He explained that he felt that an entrepreneurial bishop could enable entrepreneurial clergy in the parishes to 'punch through what is effectively a glass ceiling at the archdeacon level and make connections that actually turn out to be transformational'.

Matt spoke about the advantage he felt of being asked by the bishop to take on his current parish. He felt that having the invitation, and by extension, the backing of the bishop was 'an enabling thing'. He said, 'For somebody to say, "We, as an institution want you to go and do that job there" is massively enabling. And that's part of where I get my energy from.'

He went on to explain that he had considered the fact that, while the institution supported him in the person of the bishop, and that this was 'the episcopal system at its best', he did not feel that ongoing support was guaranteed; it was possible the senior leadership would have a change of heart. Reflecting on this, he said,

> The institution could chicken out and say, 'Actually the only way we as an institution can justify paying you a stipend is by asking you to do pastoral maintenance for an impossibly large number of people. And that's our normal mode of operation and you're not quite fitting that normal mode of operation, so I'm sorry, you're going to have to take on four more parishes or whatever and do nothing but low-level maintenance.'

Roger felt that in order for entrepreneurship to flourish at local church level it was important that the senior leadership were enabling, but that they did not need to necessarily be entrepreneurial themselves. He said,

> The clergy who are going to be entrepreneurial in their ministry need to be given the freedom to do so as well as all the other aspects of what enabling means. It's fine if your archdeacon, meanwhile, is looking after money and drains.

The responses suggest that it is possible for priests to act entrepreneurially in the parish regardless of whether or not those in senior positions, archdeacons and bishops in particular, are entrepreneurs themselves. Rupert's response suggested that it was possible for entrepreneurial area deans to use their limited influence to encourage and support an entrepreneurial approach to local church ministry in the clergy within their deanery. The presence of a non-entrepreneurial archdeacon would not in itself appear to be a particular hindrance to entrepreneurship in the parish, but an archdeacon who, rather than seeking ways to enable or encourage innovative thinking and practice, tended to ask limiting or restricting questions of ministers who were seeking to act entrepreneurially could become a block to the exercise of such entrepreneurship.

Rupert's, Dan's and Susan's responses too indicate that a non-entrepreneurial archdeacon could have a potentially dampening effect on entrepreneurship in the parish and deanery. Entrepreneurial priests who find themselves working with an archdeacon who is obstructive towards entrepreneurial efforts, rather than supportive, tolerant or even neutral, may find that they have to spend additional time and energy in finding ways to innovate in the parish. Although the respondents did not feel that the presence of a non-entrepreneurial bishop in a diocese would prevent the exercise of entrepreneurship at parish level, they felt that the presence of a bishop who demonstrated a positive attitude towards an entrepreneurial approach to priestly ministry would help to create permission, which in turn would have the effect of encouraging and enabling entrepreneurship.

From the responses, it seemed that the presence in a diocese of an overtly entrepreneurial bishop (rather than one who was sympathetic, tolerant, neutral or, at worst, obstructive towards entrepreneurship), who made it clear that an entrepreneurial approach to ministry was valued and important, could potentially create a culture of permission within the diocese which would allow entrepreneurial ministers and congregations to flourish, actively to share their experiences and to work across geographical, ecclesial, ecumenical, social and spiritual boundaries. An entrepreneurial bishop could use his or her influence to encourage a culture whereby initiative was taken and ideas generated in the diocese, and the responses indicated that such a culture might have a significant impact at parish level.

I suggest that the creation of an entrepreneurial culture in a diocese could potentially draw entrepreneurs into the system, and that it is the number of entrepreneurs in an area or region that really make the difference. A culture of permission for entrepreneurship in a diocese, in which lay and ordained ministers were encouraged and helped to recognize the importance of enabling entrepreneurship, would potentially stimulate spiritual, numerical and financial growth, draw in other entrepreneurs and create momentum for significant local and even regional transformation.

I am not suggesting that bishops should encourage the creation of a culture in which there is pressure, either stated or implied, for all ordained ministers or congregations to be entrepreneurial. However, the interview responses lead me to suggest that senior leadership can make a significant contribution to a shift towards a culture in the Church in which entrepreneurship is recognized and valued and in which entrepreneurial ministers and congregations are encouraged, supported and even rewarded, rather than discouraged, blocked, frustrated and undervalued, Whether or not they are themselves entrepreneurs, those serving the body of Christ in senior church leadership should be encouraged to consider actively pursuing a policy of encouraging entrepreneurship where it is found rather than ignoring, inhibiting or opposing it. A culture like this will be coherent with aspects of God's nature, consistent with the approach to ministry of many individuals throughout Christian history, helpful as a way of understanding the nature and purpose of Christian ministry, and appropriate in terms of addressing the missional challenge faced by the Church at this time.

Conclusion: What has been said and what do we do next?

I began this book by saying that I was an entrepreneurial Christian minister. I went on, in my Introduction, to explain that I was using the term 'entrepreneur' to refer to a way of being in the world that is characterized by a relentless and energetic pursuit of opportunities to do things in new ways in order to achieve improved outcomes for those involved. I next noted the different types of capital that entrepreneurs produce, and then articulated two central drivers for the research that underpins the book: first, my experience of being an entrepreneurial minister; and second, my understanding of the nature of the situation in which Christians are currently seeking to engage in ministry and mission. Having explained that a faithful and effective response to this situation required the contribution of entrepreneurial ministers, I pointed out the recommendation, in the report *Mission-Shaped Church*, that the Church identify and deploy 'mission entrepreneurs', and stated that the Church might profitably recognize that lay and ordained entrepreneurial ministers are a potential resource, and that it was important to identify and invest in them.

I do not suggest that all Christians should adopt an entrepreneurial approach to ministry, or that entrepreneurial ministers are a one-stop solution for the challenges currently faced by the Church. I would argue, however, that both lay and ordained entrepreneurial ministers are present in the Church, that they are able to make a positive difference as we, the people of God, seek to engage in ministry and mission. I suggest that the concept of entrepreneurship offers the Church a helpful lens through which to view the exercise of Christian ministry, and in my initial research I set out to explore the experience of a sample of ordained entrepreneurial ministers in the Diocese of Durham with a view to producing appropriate and informed suggestions for the future practice of entrepreneurship in the Church.

After the Introduction, we considered in Part 1 of the book the contested nature of the term 'entrepreneur' in relation to Christian ministry and mission. This was followed by a discussion of my definition of the entrepreneur alongside definitions proposed by Bolton and Thompson and Michael Simms. I argued that an entrepreneurial approach to ministry and mission is consistent with some of the characteristics exhibited by God, offering examples of figures in the Bible and Christian history who adopted an entrepreneurial approach to collaborating with God.

At the beginning of Part 2 I briefly discussed the methodological approach adopted in my research. This was followed by six chapters in which we considered themes emerging from data generated through online testing and semi-structured interviews. In this concluding chapter, I offer a summary of the research findings and suggestions for the exercise of entrepreneurship by lay and ordained ministers in the years ahead.

Summary of the themes that emerged from the research

When asked to articulate their feelings about using the term 'entrepreneur' in association with Christian ministry, all of the respondents were positive, although four explained that they could see why others might have an issue with such an association. Of these four, three mentioned negative associations of entrepreneurship with greed.

One respondent expressed the opinion that all ordained ministers should be entrepreneurs and another held the view that all ordained ministers should act entrepreneurially (which is a slightly different thing). One respondent spoke of his experience of feeling the need to underemphasize the entrepreneurial aspect of himself for fear of making the Church uncomfortable. Three respondents articulated the view that the Church did not appear to want entrepreneurs.

Three respondents identified positively with the word *habitually* in Bolton and Thompson's definition and of these, two also identified positively with the word *opportunities*. One respondent explained that it was important that such opportunities were spotted by entrepreneurs themselves and not by those in authority on behalf of others. The same two respondents also discussed the presence of the words *creates* and *innovates*, pointing out that in the local church setting, this didn't need to involve starting big projects from scratch or reinventing the wheel. One talked about discovering synergy and the other spoke about ministers using what they found around them and developing things to their full potential.

One respondent felt that there had always been entrepreneurs in the Church but expressed the belief that many have to leave the Church of England to achieve things. This respondent expressed a sense of frustration about entrepreneurial ventures being blocked and the apparent inability of his local church to bring about change.

Five respondents discussed issues relating to their church buildings. In their accounts it was possible to recognize some of the entrepreneurial character themes identified in the respondents' FSEI scores. In particular, I noted that respondents who talked about addressing building-related challenges by working with others and discerning ways in which creative and innovative solutions could be found regularly gained high Creativity, Advantage and Team scores.

Many ordained ministers will be required to engage with building-related issues. Analysis of the responses led me to suggest that the extent to which an ordained minister is able to identify an approach to such issues that has the potential to generate social and spiritual capital in the congregation and local community is likely to be dependent on four factors. The first of these is the minister's ability to understand that dealing with building-related issues is part of his or her task and not simply an unwelcome burden. The second is the minister's ability to see the potential for fruitful, although perhaps unusual, connections in the process of addressing building-related issues. Third is the minister's ability to facilitate a release of energy by working collaboratively and in partnership with others, in some cases by building and maintaining functional teams characterized by mutual trust and a common purpose. The fourth factor is the minister's ability to maintain a clear focus on people, both in the congregation and outside it, rather than on the building itself.

Alongside buildings, *partnering and working with others* was another prominent theme that emerged during analysis of the data. Each of the respondents talked about working with their congregations (rather than working *for* them). Three respondents talked about working with other clergy and two discussed working with bodies external to the Church. A variety of approaches to working with others were apparent in the responses, as were variations in levels of collaboration and power-sharing. Only two respondents talked about working with teams within their congregations. There was a significant contrast between the approaches of the two: one had invested significant time and effort over several years in facilitating four teams with responsibility for different areas of the life of the church, while the other discussed a single team in broad terms that did not allow a clear assessment of the extent to which the existence of the team was part of a particular strategy or whether the team had a particular remit within the life of the congregation. The first of these two respondents was the only one whose comments suggested a genuine sharing of power and influence in the congregation. This respondent also spoke about an increase in the numbers of people becoming passionate about the mission of the church and claimed that the church had grown, both numerically and spiritually.

One respondent, responsible for churches in a number of rural villages, suggested having a recognized entrepreneur in each parish rather than a recognized pastor, although he thought this might not be an effective approach in urban situations. He suggested that with some theological training, such trustworthy people in each rural parish with a local network and the respect of the community could potentially gather people around them. The respondent suggested that, as the ordained minister, he could then provide pastoral support, care and a framework for the recognized entrepreneurs. His rationale for the notion of recognized entrepreneurs in rural parishes was based first on the fact that such entrepreneurs would have local understanding and networks and second on the perceived importance of reversing the movement of power away from rural parishes and returning it to those with close ties to their communities.

It was interesting to note that the three respondents who expressed some frustration at the challenges and difficulties of working with others in the Church each had positive experiences of working in business prior to being ordained. Of these three respondents, one talked about wanting to form a team that would support him in achieving things in the parish that the church council had refused to sanction.

None of the three respondents who did not have previous experience in business expressed frustration at working within the Church. Two of these made explicit connections between love and working with members of the wider community. Both of these respondents provided examples of involvement in significant partnerships with external bodies such as the local authority. One respondent talked at length about the priority given to developing partnerships with external bodies and seeking funding from a range of sources. The two respondents who discussed partnerships with external bodies articulated a limited link between this and numerical or spiritual growth in their church.

Alongside the frustration highlighted above, it was possible to identify in the respondents' comments positive aspects of partnering and working with others, and in Chapter 7 I listed nine such positive factors (see p. 96). From their responses to questions about the factors that participants felt might aid the exercise of entrepreneurship in local churches and communities, it was possible to compile a further list of 19 factors (Chapter 8, pp. 101–2). In my view the most pertinent of these are points 5, 10, 13 and 15.

In relation to points 5 and 15, I suggest that the Church of England and other mainstream denominations should try to ensure that candidates with entrepreneurial gifts are encouraged to offer themselves for selection for 'regular' ordained ministry (rather than only as OPMs), and are then selected, trained, deployed and encouraged to minister out of their entrepreneurial ability. In relation to point 13, I suggest that any effort made within the mainstream denominations to create and sustain a 'culture of permission' would contribute to the emergence of innovative approaches to ministry and mission. In relation to point 10, and based on experience, I suggest that the regular sharing of stories (and best practice) of entrepreneurial endeavour by lay and ordained ministers and congregations stimulates further initiatives and encourages others to attempt similar things in their own contexts.

From the responses to questions about the factors that participants felt might hinder the exercise of entrepreneurship in their local church and community, it was possible to compile a list of 22 such factors (Chapter 9, pp. 106–7). In my view the most pertinent of these are points, 2, 5 and 12.

In relation to point 5, fear, whether general or specific, not only hinders the exercise of entrepreneurship but also binds individuals, congregations and entire communities, hijacks human flourishing and is entirely inconsistent with Jesus' proclamation of the kingdom. In relation to points 2 and 12, the tendency of some parts of the

institution of the Church of England and other mainstream denominations to apparently undervalue entrepreneurial gifts, previous
experience and expertise is at best foolish and unhelpful and at worst
a potentially catastrophic miscalculation of what the Church is called
to be and to do.

When asked about the extent to which the presence (or lack) of
entrepreneurship in the senior leadership at regional or national
level affected the exercise of entrepreneurship in the local church
and community, the responses suggested that participants felt it was
possible for ordained ministers to act entrepreneurially in the parish
regardless of whether or not those in senior positions, such as archdeacons and bishops, were entrepreneurs themselves. Senior leaders
(in this instance, archdeacons) who tended to ask limiting or restricting questions of ordained entrepreneurial ministers could potentially
dampen the exercise of entrepreneurship and become a drain on a
minister's entrepreneurial resources, as the minister would have to
invest additional time and energy in finding ways to innovate in spite
of the leader.

Respondents felt in contrast that an overtly entrepreneurial
bishop could encourage the taking of initiative and the generation of
ideas and that the presence of such a bishop could potentially create a
culture of permission which would allow ordained entrepreneurial
ministers and congregations to flourish, share experiences and expertise and to work across a variety of perceived boundaries.

What do we do next?

I am now going to share with you a number of suggestions for what
the Church might do next. But before that it is worth reminding
ourselves that the only worthwhile starting place for anything in
life – including, and perhaps especially, entrepreneurial approaches
to ministry – is prayer. You might like to pause for a moment and
simply give thanks to God for the gift of an entrepreneurial approach
to ministry. After this, you may feel inclined to join me in asking God
to give abundant love, humility and wisdom to all those engaged in
carrying out or facilitating an entrepreneurial approach to ministry
and mission. Alongside this it would be good to pray to the Lord
of the harvest to raise up and send out many more entrepreneurial

ministers to serve local churches and the communities in which they are placed in the decades to come.

So, then, with that prayer in our hearts, here are my 11 suggestions about what to do next.

1 Congregations, lay and ordained ministers, superintendents, bishops and those with regional and national roles should be encouraged to reassess negative perceptions of the language around entrepreneurship. Such a reassessment will aid broader recognition of the appropriateness of an entrepreneurial approach to ministry, and will assist with the emergence of a culture in the Church in which lay and ordained ministry are given greater permission for adopting an entrepreneurial approach.

2 Senior church leaders at regional and national level, along with selection secretaries, vocations advisers and those in similar or related roles, should consider ways in which a positive perception of entrepreneurship can be communicated to those demonstrating entrepreneurial flair who present themselves for consideration for ordained ministry.

3 Candidates for lay and ordained ministry with entrepreneurial flair should be sought and recruited, appropriately trained, suitably deployed and actively supported.

4 Churches should actively identify, affirm and support lay and ordained ministers who adopt an entrepreneurial approach to ministry and mission in their local churches and communities. In addition, regional church bodies such as dioceses should assist entrepreneurial ministers to network with other entrepreneurial ministers locally and nationally. They should also encourage them to share their experiences and the lessons they have learnt both locally and further afield.

5 Churches should consider creating and resourcing forums for sharing ideas, stories and best practice in relation to an entrepreneurial approach to ministry and mission. This should be recommended nationally and implemented regionally and locally.

6 Accounts of creative approaches to building-related issues and the innovative use of church buildings should be circulated regionally and nationally with the intention of assisting ministers and local congregations as they seek to discern innovative ways of approaching challenges related to their buildings.

7 Churches should encourage and support their lay and ordained entrepreneurial ministers to act as consultants to ministers and congregations who are eager to explore ways of adopting a more entrepreneurial approach to ministry and mission.

8 Lay and ordained ministers and the local churches in which they serve should be given continuing assistance and guidance in creating appropriate and effective partnerships with external bodies such as local authorities.

9 In rural deaneries and circuits, 'recognized mission entrepreneurs' should be identified, equipped, commissioned and supported in engaging in local ministry and mission.

10 Each denomination should consider the possibility of appointing a suitably experienced, qualified and networked team with a national brief in relation to entrepreneurship, ministry and mission. Such a team would focus on facilitation, encouragement, support and advocacy, as well as the enabling and sharing of ideas across dioceses, regions and denominations, the commissioning of appropriate research and publication and the dissemination of any findings.

11 Suggested avenues for further research, set out in the following pages, should be pursued and the findings disseminated for consideration and possible action by regional and national church leaders, and made available to all those involved in the selection, training and deployment of ordained ministers.

And finally . . .

The aim of this book has been to show that entrepreneurial ministers are a gift of God to the Church in every age. Entrepreneurial ministers are a particularly timely gift to the people of God in an era such as our own, one marked by rapid, discontinuous and disruptive change. As communities of Christians strive to enable, encourage and multiply the gift of entrepreneurship, we will be persistent in prayer, constant in encouragement and outward in our focus. We will work hard to deepen our discipleship, build and maintain trust and apply ourselves to collaboration and to nurturing strong teams. We will share stories of fruitfulness and good practice. We will seek out and celebrate positive entrepreneurial role models, and many of us will find fresh confidence through being given opportunities to attempt new things. We will endeavour to experience one another's churches and even other cultures as a way of broadening our horizons and grasping not just fresh ideas but an entirely new kind of creativity.

Perhaps most importantly, we will pray that each day God expands and deepens our understanding that the Holy Spirit is opening up opportunities all the time, and that part of what the Church must be about is responding to those opportunities entrepreneurially rather than ignoring or missing them. Perceiving, articulating and enabling a response to such opportunities is the task of the entrepreneurs in our midst. With this in mind we celebrate their presence and commit ourselves to working towards the emergence of a culture in the Church in which many more entrepreneurial ministers are recognized and released.

Appendix 1
Suggestions for group discussion

Introduction: Why 'entrepreneur'?

1 What are your feelings about the word 'entrepreneur'? What sort of associations and images does this word generate? Do you feel generally positive or negative towards the word? What is it about the word that prompts particular feelings?

2 Do you feel that you are an entrepreneur or have entrepreneurial ability? If so, do you feel you have been able to use these gifts in the service of the Church or the wider community? If you have, what wider factors have enabled you to feel confident about using your entrepreneurial gifts in this way? If not, why might this be?

3 Discuss your response to my statement in this chapter that 'the language of entrepreneurship offers the Church a useful lens through which to imagine the shape of mission for our emerging culture'. What 'shape' might participating in God's mission take in our culture? Does it make sense that lay and ordained ministers with entrepreneurial ability might have a particular contribution to make within this mission? What do you imagine this contribution to look like?

1 *Dragons' Den*? Towards a positive understanding of the entrepreneur

1 How do you respond to Robert Warren's assertion that 'entrepreneurs are not often team players and can be driven rather than called'?

2 Jonny Baker suggests that for those of us who remember Margaret Thatcher, the notion of entrepreneurship is 'tainted with capitalist overtones'. He goes on to say, 'it's pretty clear that it's not being used in that way in the context of mission.' Is his view reflected in your own experience?

3 Do you think there is an alternative, perhaps less contentious, word than 'entrepreneur' that might serve a similar function in the context of Christian ministry and mission? What might be gained by using this word rather than 'entrepreneur'? What might be lost?

2 Definitions of the entrepreneur

1 Consider each element of Bolton and Thompson's definition of the entrepreneur set out in this chapter. Do you recognize aspects of this definition in each other? If so, which ones?

2 Consider your own ministerial context. What kind of 'environmental' factors might encourage the emergence of more entrepreneurial ministers?

3 What specific things do you feel could be considered to encourage and facilitate an entrepreneurial approach to ministry and mission in members of the congregation of which you are a part?

3 An entrepreneurial God?

1 How do you feel about the possibility that reflection on the concept of entrepreneurship might serve to deepen our appreciation of God's character and nature?

2 Consider whether you agree with the inclusion of particular individuals in the lists of entrepreneurial characters in the Bible and Christian history. Are there others that you would add to these lists? Can you give reasons for their inclusion?

3 I have suggested that it is problematic to apply the concept of innovation to God and God's activity in the world. Discuss whether you share my reservations.

5 Feeling positive about entrepreneurs in Christian ministry

1 Roger felt that to bring the word 'entrepreneur' into the vocabulary of the Church would 'do us a lot of good'. What is your response to this claim? In what specific ways might bringing the word into the Church's vocabulary do a lot of good?

2 Matt explained that he felt the need to underemphasize the entrepreneurial aspect of his nature when going through the discernment process for ordained ministry. Discuss your responses to his claim, or reflect on the extent to which your own experiences have been like Matt's.

3 How do you respond to Susan's view that if there is not something of the entrepreneur in each ordained minister, he or she has 'no business leading community'?

6 Church buildings can be a resource

1 What are your feelings about the church buildings with which you are directly involved? Do you see potential in your church buildings, even if this potential is currently untapped?

2 How do you think your church buildings are perceived by members of the congregation and members of the wider community?

3 How might a congregation be helped to consider the various ways in which their church buildings can best serve the mission of God in a given context?

7 Teamwork and partnering with others

1 Discuss your own experiences of being part of teams or actively facilitating and supporting a team in a church context.

2 How do you respond to Rupert's suggestion of having a 'recognized entrepreneur' in each context?

3 To what extent is working in partnership, both within and beyond the church community, part of your experience of group members? You may like to share some of the lessons you have learnt as a result of working in partnership with others.

8 What factors help entrepreneurship to happen?

1 Take a few moments to reflect on the list of 19 factors that respondents suggested might aid the exercise of entrepreneurship. To which of these factors would you give greater priority, and why (see pp. 101–2)?

2 In his responses Matt talked about the importance of trust in entrepreneurial ventures. You might like to discuss some of the ways in which you would endeavour to build and maintain trust in your own contexts.

3 Rupert talked about the importance of a permission-giving culture in enabling entrepreneurship. To what extent do you believe that the presence or absence of such a culture affects the exercise of entrepreneurship at local church and community level?

9 What hinders entrepreneurship?

1 Consider the list of 22 factors that respondents felt might hinder the exercise of entrepreneurship. Do you feel that some factors are more significant than others? If so, which ones and why (see pp. 106–7)?

2 Matt claimed that the Church of England made low demands on people and that this was accompanied by low levels of personal discipleship. He suggested that both were factors that hindered entrepreneurship in the local church and community. Do you agree with Matt's point of view? If so, what do you think might be done to change this?

3 What might be done to take greater account of the experience, skills and competencies that lay and ordained ministers bring to their church roles from previous (or continuing) careers?

10 The impact of senior leadership on entrepreneurship in the local church

1 Dan talked about the need for church structures to be eased a little in order to make necessary changes in the church. You may like to reflect on your own denomination. To what extent would easing the structures enable entrepreneurship in local churches? Which aspects of the current structure might need easing? What would be gained by this? What might be lost?

2 Think about your own role within your church or denomination. In what specific ways might you be able actively to encourage and enable an entrepreneurial approach to ministry within your spheres of influence?

3 Take a few moments to reflect on those who hold leadership responsibilities in your denomination, in particular those to whom you are in some sense accountable. In what specific ways might you encourage those who occupy such roles to have a positive attitude towards entrepreneurial ministers and the exercise of entrepreneurship?

Appendix 2
Suggested essay questions

Introduction: Why 'entrepreneur'?

1 With reference to a specific example, discuss and critically evaluate the potential benefits that an ordained minister with entrepreneurial ability might bring to local church leadership.

2 With reference to a specific example, discuss and critically evaluate the contribution that lay ministers with entrepreneurial ability might make to the community beyond the church.

3 Critically evaluate the following assertion by Michael Volland: 'The language of entrepreneurship offers the church a useful lens through which to imagine the shape of mission for our emerging culture.'

1 *Dragons' Den*? Towards a positive understanding of the entrepreneur

1 With reference to appropriate literature, critically evaluate the following statement: 'The word "entrepreneur" draws together a range of qualities that, when embodied by Christians, make a pivotal contribution to God's mission in the world.'

2 Mark Casson et al. argue that popular perceptions of the entrepreneur have been shaped by the enterprise culture of the 1980s. To what extent might this be true and is the notion of entrepreneurship redeemable in the context of Christian ministry and mission?

3 With reference to appropriate literature, critically reflect on the following statement by Ian Meredith: 'I run a business as well as being active in ministry (although I don't agree with the distinction). I am entrepreneurial in both.'

2 Definitions of the entrepreneur

1 Michael Volland defines the entrepreneur as 'A visionary who, in partnership with God and others, challenges the status quo by energetically creating and innovating in order to shape something of Kingdom value'. With reference to a specific example and appropriate literature, discuss and critically evaluate this definition.

2 Michael Simms defines the 'faith entrepreneur' as 'an agent of change who adds value through creatively and passionately launching bold initiatives, all the while taking calculated risks for God'. Discuss and critically evaluate this definition with reference to a specific example and appropriate literature.
3 'Missional entrepreneurship is never a solitary venture.' Critically evaluate this statement with reference to appropriate literature and at least one example drawn from life.

3 An entrepreneurial God?

1 Drawing on appropriate literature, consider what might be gained by Christians who reflect on the possibility that God exhibits entrepreneurial qualities.
2 Critically evaluate the suggestion that applying the concept of innovation to God in any meaningful way is problematic.
3 Research one of the figures included on the list of entrepreneurs in the Bible or Christian history in this chapter. Critically consider whether your chosen character might accurately be described as an entrepreneur.

Appendix 3
Avenues for further research

My research into entrepreneurial ministers necessarily maintained a clear focus on a specific objective. However, the themes set out in Part 2 of this book suggest a number of potential avenues for further research. These are as follows:

1 An exploration of the extent to which it might be possible to alter negative perceptions of entrepreneurship in lay and ordained ministers as a result of in-depth discussion and reflection on alternative understandings of the term, rooted in a range of positive examples.

2 A study of the experience of a sample of ordained ministers, identified as entrepreneurs, during the process of discernment, selection and training for ordained ministry.

3 An exploration of how those involved in discernment and selection for ordination in the mainstream denominations understand the nature of ordained ministry and the requirements of mission in the current culture.

4 An analysis of the reasons (other than retirement or illness) why ordained ministers leave the mainstream denominations, with the aim of establishing whether entrepreneurial ministers are in fact leaving and if so, their reasons for doing so.

5 An analysis of the impact and effect on lay and ordained ministers, congregations and the wider community of significant issues related to church buildings.

6 A study of the relationship between the dissemination of power and influence in churches through teams and those churches' numerical and spiritual growth. It will also be fruitful to explore the experience, spirituality, theological position and personality type of lay and ordained ministers who have facilitated teams in their congregations.

7 An analysis of the feasibility and potential challenges, the impact and effect of identifying, releasing and supporting recognized mission entrepreneurs in rural parishes.

8 An exploration of the expectations held by those entering ordained ministry after previous careers, and the extent to which these expectations are managed and/or adapted in light of the experience of exercising ordained ministry in the Church.

9 An exploration of the relationship between church partnerships with external bodies and the creation of social and/or spiritual capital in the wider community. And also between partnerships with external bodies and growth (both spiritual and numerical), in church congregations.

10 A study of the approaches that lay and ordained ministers adopt in working with congregations, other ministers, local communities and external bodies. It will be helpful to study the effect of different approaches to working with others over time and in a range of contexts, and to identify and evaluate the factors that prompt and enable ministers to work with others and those that keep them from doing so.

11 A study of the extent to which the presence of factors identified as aiding the exercise of an entrepreneurial approach to ministry in a local church or community can be discerned and evaluated in churches that demonstrate an entrepreneurial approach to ministry and mission. It will also be interesting to reflect on the presence or absence, in churches demonstrating an entrepreneurial approach, of factors identified as hindering the exercise of an entrepreneurial approach to ministry in a local church or community.

12 A study of the extent to which the presence of factors identified as hindering the exercise of an entrepreneurial approach to ministry in a local church or community may be discerned and evaluated in churches whose congregations are declining numerically, who are lacking engagement with the local community, or are experiencing a general sense of confusion or financial difficulties.

13 An interesting (and potentially ethically challenging) avenue for further research will be an exploration of the relationship between the presence of entrepreneurial and non-entrepreneurial senior leaders (including bishops and archdeacons) and the effect on the exercise of entrepreneurship in their dioceses or

other areas of responsibility. Such a study will take account of the presence of lay and ordained entrepreneurial ministers and will need to adopt a comparative methodology, perhaps studying a diocese or other area over time and alongside one or more equivalent areas.

Bibliography and further reading

Adair, John, *Effective Leadership: How to Grow Leaders: The Seven Key Principles of Effective Leadership Development* (London: Kogan Page, 2005).

Adair, John, *Effective Innovation: The Essential Guide to Staying Ahead of the Competition* (London: Pan Books, 2009).

Adair, John, *Effective Leadership: How to be a Successful Leader* (London: Pan, 2009).

Adair, John, *Leadership for Innovation: How to Organize Team Creativity and Harvest Ideas* (London: Kogan Page, 2009).

Adair, John, et al., *101 Great Ideas for Growing Healthy Churches* (London: Canterbury Press, 2012).

Adair, John and John Nelson (eds), *Creative Church Leadership* (London: Canterbury Press, 2004).

Allen, Diogenes, *Christian Belief in a Postmodern World: The Full Wealth of Conviction* (Louisville, KY: Westminster John Knox Press, 1989).

Amabile, Teresa M., 'Motivating Creativity in Organizations: On Doing What You Love and Loving What You Do', *California Management Review*, 40:1 (1997), 39–58.

The Archbishop's Council, *Breaking New Ground: Church Planting in the Church of England* (London: Church House Publishing, 1994).

The Archbishop's Council, *Mission-Shaped Church: Church Planting and Fresh Expression of Church in a Changing Context* (London: Church House Publishing, 2004).

The Archbishop's Council and the Trustees for Methodist Church Purposes, *Fresh Expressions in the Mission of the Church: Report of an Anglican–Methodist Working Party* (London: Church House Publishing, 2012).

Armstrong, Regis J., *Clare of Assisi: The Lady* (New York: New City Press, 2006).

Atavar, Michael, *Everyone is Creative* (London: Kiosk Publishing, 2013).

Avis, Paul, *The Anglican Understanding of the Church: An Introduction* (London: SPCK, 2000).

Babbie, Earl, *The Practice of Social Research*, 11th edn (Belmont, CA: Thomson Higher Education, 2007).

Ballard, Paul and John Pritchard, *Practical Theology in Action* (London: SPCK, 1996).

Barbour, Rosaline, *Introducing Qualitative Research: A Student's Guide to the Craft of Doing Qualitative Research* (London: Sage, 2008).

Bartlett, Alan, *A Passionate Balance: The Anglican Tradition* (London: Darton, Longman and Todd, 2007).

Bayes, Paul and Tim Sledge, *Mission-Shaped Parish: Traditional Church in a Changing Context* (London: Church House Publishing, 2006).

Bell, Judith, *Doing Your Research Project: A Guide for First-Time Researchers in Education, Health and Social Science*, 5th edn (Maidenhead: McGraw-Hill Education, 2010).

Bevans, Stephen B. and Roger P. Schroeder, *Constants in Context: A Theology of Mission for Today* (New York: Orbis Books, 2004).

Bolton, Bill, *The Entrepreneur and the Church*, Grove Pastoral Series, P107 (Cambridge: Grove Books, 2006).

Bolton, Bill and John Thompson, *The Entrepreneur in Focus: Achieve Your Potential* (London: Thomson, 2003).

Bolton, Bill and John Thompson, *Entrepreneurs: Talent, Temperament, Technique*, 2nd edn (Oxford: Elsevier Butterworth-Heinemann, 2004).

Booth, Wayne C., Gregory G. Colomb and Joseph M. Williams, *The Craft of Research*, 3rd edn (Chicago: University of Chicago Press, 2008).

Bosch, David J., *Transforming Mission: Paradigm Shifts in Theology of Mission* (New York: Orbis Books, 1991).

Brafman, Ori and Rod A. Beckstrom, *The Starfish and the Spider: The Unstoppable Power of Leaderless Organizations* (New York: Penguin, 2006).

Breen, Mike, *Building a Discipline Culture* (Pawleys Island, SC: 3 Dimension Ministries, 2011).

Brockhaus, Robert H. et al. (eds), *Entrepreneurship Education: A Global View* (Aldershot: Ashgate Publishing, 2001).

Brueggemann, Walter, *The Prophetic Imagination*, 2nd edn (Minneapolis, MN: Augsburg Fortress, 2001).

Caird, Sally, 'The Enterprising Tendency of Occupational Groups', *International Small Business Journal* 9:4 (1991), 75–81.

Cameron, Helen et al., *Talking About God in Practice: Theological Action Research and Practical Theology* (London: SCM Press, 2010).

Carey, S. Pearce and Peter Masters, *William Carey* (London: Wakeman Trust, 1993).

Carr, Wesley, *The Priestlike Task* (London: SPCK, 1985).

Casson, Mark, *The Entrepreneur: An Economic Theory* (Oxford: Martin Robertson, 1982).

Casson, Mark et al. (eds), *The Oxford Handbook of Entrepreneurship* (Oxford: Oxford University Press, 2008).

Checkland, Sydney George, *The Rise of Industrial Society in England 1815–1885* (London: Longmans, Green & Co., 1964).

Chell, Elizabeth et al., *The Entrepreneurial Personality: Concepts, Cases and Categories* (London: Routledge, 1991).

Cocksworth, Christopher and Rosaline Brown, *Being a Priest Today: Exploring Priestly Identity* (Norwich: Canterbury Press, 2002).

Cohen, Louis, Lawrence Manion and Keith Morrison, *Research Methods in Education*, 6th edn (Abingdon: Routledge, 2007).

Cole, Neil, *Organic Church: Growing Faith Where Life Happens* (San Francisco, CA: Jossey-Bass, 2005).

Collins, Jim, *Good to Great* (London: Random House, 2001).

Common Worship: Services and Prayers for the Church of England (London: Church House Publishing, 2000).

Corrie, John (ed.), *Dictionary of Mission Theology: Evangelical Foundations* (Nottingham: Inter-Varsity Press, 2007).

Covey, Stephen R., *The 7 Habits of Highly Effective People: Powerful Lessons in Personal Change* (London: Simon & Schuster, 2004).

Creswell, John W., *Research Design: Qualitative, Quantitative, and Mixed Methods Approaches*, 3rd edn (London: Sage, 2009).

Croft, Steven, *Ministry in Three Dimensions: Ordination and Leadership in the Local Church*, revised edn (London: Darton, Longman and Todd, 2008).

Croft, Steven and Ian Mobsby, *Ancient Faith, Future Mission: Fresh Expressions in the Sacramental Tradition* (London: Canterbury Press, 2009).

Croft, Steven (ed.), *Evangelism in a Spiritual Age: Communicating Faith in a Changing Culture* (London: Church House Publishing, 2005).

Croft, Steven (ed.), *The Future of the Parish System: Shaping the Church of England for the Twenty-first Century* (London: Church House Publishing, 2006).

Croft, Steven (ed.), *Mission-Shaped Questions: Defining Issues for Today's Church* (London: Church House Publishing, 2008).

Czarniawska, Barbara, *Narratives in Social Science Research* (London: Sage, 2004).

Davie, Grace, *Religion in Britain Since 1945: Believing Without Belonging* (Oxford: Blackwell, 1994).

Davis, Oliver, *The Creativity of God: World, Eucharist, Reason* (Cambridge: Cambridge University Press, 2004).

Dawson, Catherine, *Introduction to Research Methods* (Oxford: How to Books, 2009).

Delmar, Frederic and Frederic C. Witte, 'The Psychology of the Entrepreneur', in Sarah Carter and Dylan Jones-Evans (eds), *Enterprise and Small Business: Principles, Practice and Policy* (Harlow: Prentice Hall, 2000).

Denscombe, Martyn, *The Good Research Guide: For Small-Scale Social Research Projects*, 3rd edn (Maidenhead: Open University Press, 2007).

Denzin, Norman K. and Yvonna S. Lincoln (eds), *Collecting and Interpreting Qualitative Materials*, 2nd edn (Thousand Oaks, CA: Sage, 1998).

Doornenbal, Robert, *Crossroads: An Exploration of the Emerging Missional Conversation with a Special Focus on 'Missional Leadership' and its Challenges for Theological Education* (Delft: Eburon Academic, 2012).

Drane, John, *Cultural Change and Biblical Faith: The Future of the Church. Biblical and Missiological Essays for the New Century* (Carlisle: Paternoster Press, 2000).

Drucker, Peter F., *The New Realities* (London: Heinemann, 1989).

Drucker, Peter F., *Innovation and Entrepreneurship* (Oxford: Butterworth-Heinemann, 2007).

Elkington, John and Pamela Hartigan, *The Power of Unreasonable People: How Social Entrepreneurs Create Markets That Change the World* (Harvard: Harvard Business School Press, 2008).

Fiddes, Paul S., *Participating in God: A Pastoral Doctrine of the Trinity* (London: Darton, Longman and Todd, 2000).

Fisher, James L. and James V. Koch, *Born not Made: The Entrepreneurial Personality* (Westport, CT: Praeger Publishers, 2008).

Frost, Michael, *Exiles: Living Missionally in Post Christian Culture* (Peabody, MA: Hendrickson, 2006).

Frost, Michael and Alan Hirsch, *The Shaping of Things to Come* (Peabody, MA: Hendrickson, 2003).

Frost, Rob, David Wilkinson and Joanne Cox (eds), *The Call and the Commission: Equipping a New Generation of Leaders For a New World* (Carlisle: Paternoster Press, 2009).

Gay, Doug, *Remixing the Church: Towards and Emerging Ecclesiology* (London: SCM Press, 2011).

Gibb, Allan A., 'Entrepreneurship and Intrapreneurship – Exploring the Differences', in R. Donckels and A. Miettinen (eds), *New Findings and Perspectives in Entrepreneurship* (Aldershot: Gower, 1990).

Gibbs, Eddie and Ryan Bolger, *Emerging Churches* (London: SPCK, 2006).

Gibson, William J. and Andrew Brown, *Working with Qualitative Data* (London: Sage, 2009).

Goodhew, David, Andrew Roberts and Michael Volland, *Fresh: An Introduction to Fresh Expressions of Church and Pioneer Ministry* (London: SCM Press, 2012).

Goodhew, David (ed.), *Church Growth in Britain: 1980 to the Present* (Farnham: Ashgate Publishing, 2012).

Greenwood, Robin, *Transforming Priesthood: A New Theology of Mission and Ministry* (London: SPCK, 1994).

Greenwood, Robin, *Being Church: The Formation of Christian Community* (London: SPCK, 2013).

Grundy, Malcolm, *Leadership and Oversight: New Models for Episcopal Ministry* (London: Mowbray, 2011).

Handy, Charles, *The Age of Unreason: New Thinking for a New World*, 2nd edn (London: Random House, 2002).

Harding, Jamie, *Qualitative Data Analysis From Start to Finish* (London: Sage, 2013).

Harrer, Heinrich, *The White Spider: The Story of the North Face of the Eiger* (London: Harper Perennial, 2005).

Harvard Business Review on Entrepreneurship (Boston: HBS Press, 1999).

Harvard Business Review on Innovation (Boston: HBS Press, 2001).

Hattersley, Roy, *Blood and Fire: William and Catherine Booth and the Salvation Army* (London: Abacus, 1999).

Healy, Nicholas M., *Church, World and the Christian Life: Practical-Prophetic Ecclesiology* (Cambridge: Cambridge University Press, 2000).

Heaton, Janet, *Reworking Qualitative Data* (London: Sage, 2004).

Hebert, Robert F. and Albert N. Link, *The Entrepreneur: Mainstream Views and Radical Critiques* (New York: Praeger, 1988).

Hegarty, John, *Hegarty on Creativity: There are no Rules* (London: Thames and Hudson, 2014).

Hennink, Monique, Inge Hutter and Ajay Bailey, *Qualitative Research Methods* (London: Sage, 2011).

Herman, Luc and Bart Vervaeck, *Handbook of Narrative Analysis* (Lincoln and London: University of Nebraska Press, 2005).

Hirsch, Alan and Lance Ford, *Right Here, Right Now: Everyday Mission for Everyday People* (Grand Rapids, MI: Baker Books, 2011).

Hirsch, Alan and Tim Catchim, *The Permanent Revolution: Apostolic Imagination and Practice for the 21st Century Church* (San Francisco, CA: Jossey-Bass, 2012).

Hisrich, Robert D. and Michael P. Peters, *Entrepreneurship: Starting, Developing and Managing a New Enterprise* (Homewood, IL: Irwin, 1992).

Hockerts, Jeffery, Kai Mair and Johanna Robinson (eds), *Social Entrepreneurship* (Palgrave Macmillan, 2005).

Hockerts, Jeffery, Kai Mair, and Johanna Robinson (eds), *Values and Opportunities in Social Entrepreneurship* (Basingstoke: Palgrave Macmillan, 2010).

Hollinghurst, Steve, *Mission-Shaped Evangelism: The Gospel in Contemporary Culture* (London: Canterbury Press, 2010).

Honey, Peter and Alan Mumford, *The Manual of Learning Styles* (London: Peter Honey Publications, 1986).

Hoselitz, Bert, 'The Early History of Entrepreneurial Theory', *Explorations in Entrepreneurial History* 3 (1951).

Hughes, Jonathan, *The Vital Few* (Oxford: Oxford University Press, 1973).

Hull, John, *Mission-Shaped Church: A Theological Response* (London: SCM Press, 2006).

Isaac, Les and Rosalind Davies, *Faith on the Streets: Christians in Action Through the Street Pastors Movement* (London: Hodder & Stoughton, 2014).

Isba, Anne, *The Excellent Mrs Fry: The Unlikely Heroine* (London: Continuum Books, 2010).

Jackson, Bob, *The Road to Growth: Towards a Thriving Church* (London: Church House Publishing, 2005).

Johnson, Spencer, *Who Moved My Cheese?* (London: Vermilion, 1999).

Johnson, Steven, *Where Good Ideas Come From: The Natural History of Innovation* (London: Penguin, 2010).

Kagawa, Toyohiko, *Living Out Christ's Love*, Upper Room Spiritual Classics Series 2 (London: Upper Room Books, 1998).

Kanter, Rosabeth M., *The Change Masters: Corporate Entrepreneurs at Work* (London: Unwin, 1984).

Kao, Raymond W., *An Entrepreneurial Approach to Corporate Management* (London: Prentice Hall, 1997).

Kilby, Peter M. (ed.), *Entrepreneurship and Economic Development* (New York: Macmillan, 1971).

Kim, Philip H. and Howard E. Aldrich, 'Social Capital and Entrepreneurship', *Foundations and Trends in Entrepreneurship* 1:2 (2005).

Kirby, David A., 'Developing Graduate Entrepreneurs: The UK Graduate Enterprise Programme', *Entrepreneurship, Innovation and Change* 1:2 (1992), 165–75.

Kirby, David A., *Entrepreneurship* (Maidenhead: McGraw-Hill Education, 2003).

Kirby, David A. and David Mullen, 'Developing Enterprising Undergraduates', *Journal of European Industrial Training* 14:2 (1989), 27–32.

Kirzner, Israel M., *Competition and Entrepreneurship* (Chicago: University of Chicago Press, 1973).

Knight, Frank H., *Risk, Uncertainty and Profit* (Boston: Houghton Mifflin, 1921).

Kolb, Deborah A., *Experiential Learning* (Englewood Cliffs, NJ: Prentice Hall, 1984).

Kuratko, Donald F. and Richard M. Hodgetts, *Entrepreneurship: A Contemporary Approach*, 5th edn (Sydney: Harcourt College Publishers, 2001).

Landes, David S., Joel Mokyr and William J. Baumol (eds.), *The Invention of Enterprise: Entrepreneurship from Ancient Mesopotamia to Modern Times* (Princeton, NJ: Princeton University Press, 2010).

Lawrence, James, *Growing Leaders: Reflections on Leadership, Life and Jesus* (Oxford: Bible Reading Fellowship, 2004).

Light, Paul C., *The Search for Social Entrepreneurship* (New York: Brookings Institution, 2008).

Livesay, Harold C., 'Entrepreneurial History', in Calvin A. Kent, Donald L. Sexton and Karl H. Vesper (eds), *Encyclopedia of Entrepreneurship* (Englewood Cliffs, NJ: Prentice-Hall, 1982).

McClelland, David C., *The Achieving Society* (Princeton, NJ: Van Nostrand, 1961).

MacCulloch, Diarmaid, *A History of Christianity: The First Three Thousand Years* (London: Penguin, 2010).

McNiff, Jean and Jack Whitehead, *Doing and Writing Action Research* (London: Sage, 2009).

Male, Dave (ed.), *Pioneers for Life: Explorations in Theology and Wisdom for Pioneering Leaders* (Abingdon: Bible Reading Fellowship, 2011).

The Ministry Division of the Archbishop's Council, *Formation for Ministry Within a Learning Church. Shaping the Future: New Patterns of Training for Lay and Ordained* (London: Church House Publishing, 2006).

Mobsby, Ian J., *Emerging and Fresh Expressions of Church: How Are They Authentically Church and Anglican?* (London: Moot Community Publishing, 2007).

Moynagh, Michael, *Changing World, Changing Church: New Forms of Church* (London: Monarch Books, 2001).

Moynagh, Michael, *Church for Every Context: An Introduction to Theology and Practice* (London: SCM Press, 2012).

Moynagh, Michael, *Being Church, Doing Life: Creating Gospel Communities Where Life Happens* (Oxford: Monarch Books, 2014).

Murray, Stuart, *Church After Christendom* (Carlisle: Paternoster Press, 2004).

Murray, Stuart, *Post-Christendom: Church and Mission in a Strange New World* (Carlisle: Paternoster Press, 2004).

Myers, Joseph R., *Organic Community* (Grand Rapids: Baker Books, 2007).

Nelson, John, Michael Lofthouse and Anton Muller, *101 Great Ideas for Growing Healthy Churches* (London: Canterbury Press, 2012).

Nelstrop, Louise and Martyn Percy (eds), *Evaluating Fresh Expressions: Explorations in Emerging Church. Responses to the Changing Face of Ecclesiology in the Church of England* (London: Canterbury Press, 2008).

Newbigin, Lesslie, *The Gospel in a Pluralist Society* (London: SPCK, 1989).

Nicholls, Alex (ed.), *Social Entrepreneurship: New Models of Sustainable Social Change* (Oxford: Oxford University Press, 2008).

O'Loughlin, Thomas, *Saint Patrick: The Man and his Works* (London: SPCK, 1999).

Peters, Tom, *Thriving on Chaos: Handbook for a Management Revolution* (London: Pan Books, 1987).

Peters, Tom, *Re-Imagine! Business Excellence in a Disruptive Age* (London: Dorling Kindersley, 2009).

Pritchard, John, *The Life and Work of a Priest* (London: SPCK, 2007).

Rae, David M., 'Teaching Entrepreneurship in Asia: Impact of Pedagogical Innovation', *Entrepreneurship, Innovation and Change* 6:3 (1997), 193–227.

Rae, David M., *Entrepreneurship: From Opportunity to Action* (Basingstoke: Palgrave Macmillan, 2007).

Ramsey, Michael, *The Christian Priest Today*, revised edn (London: SPCK, 1985).

Read, Stuart et al., *Effectual Entrepreneurship* (Abingdon: Routledge, 2011).

Redfern, Alastair, *Being Anglican* (London: Darton, Longman and Todd, 2004).

Riessman, Catherine K., *Narrative Methods for the Human Sciences* (London: Sage, 2008).

Robson, Colin, *Real World Research: A Resource for Social Scientists and Practitioner-Researchers* (Oxford: Blackwell, 1993).

Robson, Michael J. P., *The Cambridge Companion to Francis of Assisi* (Cambridge: Cambridge University Press, 2011).

Rothwell, Roy, 'Innovation and Firm Size: A Case for Dynamic Complementarity; or is Small really Beautiful?' *Journal of General Management* 8:3 (1983), 5–25.

Rowland, Deborah and Malcolm Higgs, *Sustaining Change: Leadership that Works* (San Francisco, CA: Jossey-Bass, 2008).

Roxburgh, Alan J., *Missional Map-Making: Skills for Leading in Times of Transition* (San Francisco, CA: Jossey-Bass, 2010).

Roxburgh, Alan J., *Missional: Joining God in the Neighborhood* (Grand Rapids, MI: Baker Books, 2011).

Roxburgh, Alan J. and Fred Romanuk, *The Missional Leader: Equipping Your Church to Reach a Changing World* (San Francisco, CA: Jossey-Bass, 2006).

Sarachek, Bernard, 'American Entrepreneurs and the Horatio Alger Myth', *Journal of Economic History* 38 (1978), 439–56.

Sarasvathy, Saras D., *Effectuation: Elements of Entrepreneurial Expertise* (Cheltenham: Edward Elgar Publishing, 2008).

Savage, Sarah and Eolene Boyd-Macmillan, *The Human Face of the Church: A Social Psychology and Pastoral Theology Resource for Pioneer and Traditional Ministry* (London: Canterbury Press, 2007).

Schumpeter, Joseph A., *The Theory of Economic Development* (Harvard: Harvard University Press, 1911, reprinted 1934).

Schumpeter, Joseph A., *Capitalism, Socialism, and Democracy* (New York: Harper and Brothers, 1942).

Sedgwick, Peter, *The Enterprise Culture: A Challenging New Theology of Wealth Creation for the 1990s* (London: SPCK, 1992).

Shane, Scott, *A General Theory of Entrepreneurship: The Individual–Opportunity Nexus* (Cheltenham: Edward Elgar, 2003).

Shier-Jones, Angela, *Pioneer Ministry and Fresh Expressions of Church* (London: SPCK, 2009).

Silverman, David, *Doing Qualitative Research*, 3rd edn (London: Sage, 2010).

Simms, Michael K., *Faith Entrepreneurs: Empowering People by Faith, Nonprofit Organizational Leadership, and Entrepreneurship* (Lincoln, NE: iUniverse, 2006).

Spencer, Nick, *Parochial Vision: The Future of the English Parish* (Carlisle: Paternoster Press, 2004).

Standing, Roger (ed.), *As a Fire by Burning: Mission as the Life of the Local Congregation* (London: SCM Press, 2013).

Stevenson, Howard H. and David E. Gumpert, 'The Heart of Entrepreneurship', *Harvard Business Review* (March–April 1985), 85–94.

Swedberg, Richard (ed.), *Entrepreneurship: The Social Science View* (Oxford: Oxford University Press, 2000).

Swinton, John and Harriet Mowatt, *Practical Theology and Qualitative Research* (London: SCM Press, 2006).

Sykes, Stephen, John Booty and Jonathan Knight, *The Study of Anglicanism* (London: SPCK, 1998).

Teresa of Ávila (translated by J. M. Cohen), *The Life of Saint Teresa of Ávila by Herself* (London: Penguin Classics, 1987).

Tickle, Phyllis, *Emergence Christianity: What it is, Where it is Going, and Why it Matters* (Grand Rapids, MI: Baker Books, 2012).

Timmons, Jeffry A., *The Entrepreneurial Mind* (Andover, MA: Brick House Publishing, 1989).

Tomkins, Stephen, *John Wesley: A Biography* (London: Lion Books, 2003).

Torry, Malcolm (ed.), *The Parish. People, Place and Ministry: A Theological and Practical Exploration* (London: Canterbury Press, 2004).

Van Gelder, Craig, and Dwight J. Zscheile, *The Missional Church in Perspective: Mapping Trends and Shaping the Conversation* (Grand Rapids, MI: Baker Academic, 2011).

Volland, Michael, *Through the Pilgrim Door: Pioneering a Fresh Expression of Church* (Eastbourne: Survivor, 2009).

Von Hayek, Friedrich A., 'Economics and Knowledge', *Economica*, new series, 4 (1937), 33–54.

Von Mises, Ludwig, *Human Action: A Treatise on Economics* (London: Hodge, 1949).

Walker, Andrew, *Telling the Story: Gospel, Mission and Culture* (London: SPCK, 1996).

Walker, Simon P., *Leading Out of Who You Are: Discovering the Secret of Undefended Leadership* (Carlisle: Piquant Editions, 2007).

Walker, Simon P., *Leading With Nothing to Lose: Training in the Exercise of Power* (Carlisle: Piquant Editions, 2007).

Walker, Simon P., *Leading With Everything to Give: Lessons from the Success and Failure of Western Capitalism* (Carlisle: Piquant Editions, 2009).

Ward, Frances, *Lifelong Learning: Theological Education and Supervision* (London: SCM Press, 2005).

Ward, Pete, *Liquid Church* (Carlisle: Paternoster Press, 2002).

Ward, Pete, *Participation and Mediation: A Practical Theology for the Liquid Church* (London: SCM Press, 2008).

Weber, Robert E., *Ancient-Future Faith: Rethinking Evangelicalism for a Postmodern World* (Grand Rapids, MI: Baker Books, 1999).

Wells, Samuel and Sarah Coakley (eds), *Praying for England: Priestly Presence in Contemporary Culture* (London: Continuum, 2008).

Wheatley, Margaret J., *Leadership and the New Science: Discovering Order in a Chaotic World*, 3rd edn (San Francisco, CA: Berrett-Koehler Publishers, 2006).

Wickham, Philip A., *Strategic Entrepreneurship: A Decision-Making Approach to New Venture Creation and Management* (London: Pitman Publishing, 1998).

Williams, Rowan, *On Christian Theology* (Oxford: Blackwell, 2000).

Wright, Christopher J. H., *The Mission of God: Unlocking the Bible's Grand Narrative* (Nottingham: Inter-Varsity Press, 2006).

Wright, N. T., *The New Testament and the People of God* (London: SPCK, 1992).

Wright, N. T., *Jesus and the Victory of God* (London: SPCK, 2004).

Wright, Walter C., *Relational Leadership: A Biblical Model for Leadership Service* (Milton Keynes: Paternoster Press, 2000).

Index

Rupert (area dean with
two rural parishes)
74, 82 n1; aids to
entrepreneurship
100, 127; hindrances
to entrepreneurship
105; impact of senior
leadership 105,
112–13, 114; positive
about entrepreneurs
75; teamwork and
partnership 84, 85, 86,
88–9, 96, 97, 127
rural parishes 39, 119,
123, 132
Ruth 61

Salvation Army 63
sanctification 57
Schumpeter, Joseph 23–4,
29–30, 30 n62, 37, 57
Scripture, relating to 8
Second Order of St
Francis 63
Sedgwick, Peter 17
senior leadership, impact
on entrepreneurship
94–5, 99, 100, 105,
111–15, 121, 128,
132–3
Sermon on the Mount
20–1
Siegel, Jordan I. 24–5
Simms, Michael 38–40,
42–3, 45, 46, 117,
130
social capital 44–5, 58–9,
82, 83, 93, 103, 107,
118, 132
Social, theme 71, 72
solidarity 16
Southwell diocese 34
n1, 72
spiritual capital 1, 45, 82,
118, 132
spiritual entrepreneur 17

status quo, challenging 3,
32, 51, 129
strategy 98, 99
Street Pastors 64
Susan (vicar, large
suburban parish)
74, 82 n1; aids to
entrepreneurship 98,
100–1; hindrances
to entrepreneurship
105–6; impact of
senior leadership 105,
111, 114; positive
about entrepreneurs
76, 126; teamwork and
partnership 84, 85,
91–2, 93, 96, 97
Sutton, Jane 16
Swedberg, Richard 23, 26,
30 n62
synergy 118

talent 35, 42, 45, 72
Team, theme 71–2, 80, 82
n1, 82–3, 118
teamwork and
partnership 3, 32, 51,
83, 84–97, 118–19,
120, 123, 127, 129;
with God 51–2;
negative factors 95–6;
positive factors 96
temperament 72
tenacity 99, 102
Teresa of Ávila, St 63
Thatcher, Margaret 17,
18, 125
*Theory of Economic
Development, The*
(Schumpeter) 30
Thompson, John 7, 26, 30,
31, 34–6, 51–60, 71–2,
82–3, 100, 117, 126
*Tractatus Logico-
Philosophicus*
(Wittgenstein) 47–8

trust 98, 101, 127

Ucbasaran, Deniz 39
uncertainty 29
undertaker 28

value *see* kingdom value,
shaping things of;
recognized value,
building things of
vision 94, 95, 98, 101
visionary 3, 32, 51, 88,
100, 129; God as 51–2
vocation 79, 106
volunteers 85, 87, 88
von Hayek, Friedrich
A. 41
von Zinzendorf, Nikolaus
Ludwig, Count 63

'walking beside people'
93
Warren, Rick 64
Warren, Robert 17, 125
wealth creation 15, 17,
19–23, 24
wealthy, the 21
Welby, Justin, Bishop of
Durham 70
Wells, Sam 10 n14
Went, John 16
Wesley, John 63
Westhead, Paul 39
White Spider, The
(Harrer) 41
Wife of Noble Character
61
Wilkinson, David 16
Wilson, Ann Marie 64
Wittgenstein, Ludwig 47
Wright, Mike 39
Wright, Tom 21

YHWH *see* God

Zacchaeus 20, 21

Did you know that SPCK is a registered charity?

As well as publishing great books by leading Christian authors, we also . . .

. . . **make assemblies meaningful and fun for over a million children** by running www.assemblies.org.uk, a popular website that provides free assembly scripts for teachers. For many children, school assembly is the only contact they have with Christian faith and culture, and the only time in their week for spiritual reflection.

. . . **help prisoners become confident readers** with our easy-to-read stories. Poor literacy is a huge barrier to rehabilitation. Prisoners identify with the believable heroes of our gritty fiction, but questions at the end of each chapter help them to examine their choices from a moral perspective and to build their reading confidence.

. . . **support student ministers overseas in their training**. We give them free, specially written theology books, the International Study Guides. These books really do make a difference, not just to students but to ministers and, through them, to a whole community.

Please support these great schemes: visit www.spck.org.uk/support-us to find out more.